水流柔術

Mizu Ryu Ju Jutsu Student Manual – Book 1

Syllabus and additional material
By Anthony J Bailey, 7th Dan Ju Jutsu
© All content copyright A. Bailey 2023

Est. 24th April 1994

Anthony Bailey

I always thought I could rely on my punching and kicking skill to end a fight. Attending a seminar with Sensei Tony teaching, really opened my eyes to other techniques which were far more effective than I previously understood. Learning about pressure points too, has opened up a new way of looking at my own art, as well as some good, but painful lessons. Much respect to you Sir!

M. Vermont, Sensei – 4th Dan Shotokan Karate

This man has a wealth of knowledge. A wonderful man. He made it look so easy, yet was strong, fast and controlled. A great teacher and experienced fighter. If you ever get the chance to train under this man, do it, you don't know what you're missing.

K. Priestly, Shihan – 7th Dan Kyokushin Karate

In life, there are few instructors who really care and have the high standards of integrity you have……..A true master of the arts……..and if I ever had to face you in a fight, I'd shoot you at a distance. Wouldn't risk the chance of getting close!

K. Mills, Kyoshi – 7th Dan Kenpo Karate

Lovely man. He's my friend. He's F***ing dangerous and I love it!

R. Woodard, Hanshi – 9th Dan Karate

Do not underestimate him. I have travelled around the globe teaching Martial Arts over the last 50 years and can say that Anthony is one of the best Ju Jitsu Instructors not just in this country, but in the world.

Brian M Dossett, Soke – 10th Dan Ju Jitsu

Mizu Ryu Ju Jutsu

Syllabus and additional material
By Anthony J Bailey, 7th Dan Ju Jutsu
© All content copyright A. Bailey 2023

Books in the Mizu Ryu Ju Jutsu Manual series

Student Manual – Book 1 (History, syllabus requirements & Kuden)
Technical Manual – Book 2 (Techniques of Mizu Ryu Ju Jutsu syllabus)

ISBN 9798867840488

Acknowledgements

Dedicated to my children, Lewis, Miya and Sofia and the Late, Great Phenom, Pope Pillagius.

My thanks go to my long-term club Instructors at Basingstoke Ju Jutsu Club: Andy, Steve, Wayne, Matthew, Tom and Katie, without whom, we would not have survived.

Thank you to the many students I've had the pleasure of sharing knowledge with over the decades and to my teachers: Sensei's Derek Brownett, Len Dunce, Ron Peploe, Soke Dossett, Sue Norman, Paul Masters Shike, my Mum and Dad, Ric Lovett and countless street opponents, who all influenced different aspects of my education with knowledge and experiences I pass on to others.

Contents

Introduction p11
History of Mizu Ryu Ju Jutsu p13
Mizu Ryu Ju Jutsu Syllabus p21
    Tying the belt p22
    White Belt p23
    Core Kihons p24
    9th Kyu Red Belt p25
    8th Kyu Yellow Belt p27
    7th Kyu Orange Belt p29
    6th – 5th Kyu Green Belt p31
    4th – 3rd Kyu Blue Belt p35
    2nd – 1st Kyu Brown Belt p38
    Shodan – Black Belt 1st Dan p41

The Hakama p44
Atemiwaza Terminology p46
Bokken Kenjutsu p 47
Technique Application p49
Senpai and Kohai p51
Notes p52

Supplemental Information p53
    Ceremonial Grades p54
    Happo no Kuzushi p55
    Triangle Theory p56
    Yielding p57
    Yin & Yang p58
    Quadrant Theory p59
    Superglue Theory p60
    Newton's Laws of Motion p61
    Mokuso p62
    Mandala p65
    Reiki p66
    5 Element Theory p68
    Points and Meridians in Martial Arts p70
    Technique Enhancers p71
    Points in Kihons p72
    The Diurnal Cycle p73
    Colour as a 'Player' p74
    12 Main Meridians p75
    Notes p87

Kuden p87
- Perseverance and The Koi p88
- Philosophy of Mizu Ryu Ju Jutsu p89
- Calligraphy and translation by Takase Shihan p90
- Buddhism and Martial Arts p93
- Fudo Myo-o p94
- Kuji-Ho p95
- Shu Ha Ri p96
- Gokai Sansho p97
- Situational Awareness p98
- Keeping Children Safe p100
- Problem-Solving Tools p107
- Learning styles & Autism p130
- Mental Training p136
- Martial States of Mind p138
- Intent p140
- Zanshin p142
- Masakatsu Agatsu p145
- Wabi-Sabi p149
- Martial Equilibrium Part 1 p151
- Martial Equilibrium Part 2 p155
- Martial Equilibrium Part 3 p160
- The Stonemason p163
- Ikigai p165
- Mizu Shin p168

Mizu Ryu Ju Jutsu Emblem p169
Haiku of Mizu Ryu Ju Jutsu p170
Mandala for Colouring p171
Notes p177

Introduction from the Founder

This book is not only a good foundation into studying the history and syllabus of Mizu Ryu Ju Jutsu, but it also sets out detailed information on the meaning behind each of the different colour belts in the grading syllabus as well as some of the teachings usually only covered in private tuition.

Mizu Ryu Ju Jutsu is a Gendai Nihon Ju Jutsu style, a modern Japanese style of Ju Jutsu. It is not Koryu, having been consecrated in 1994 and although we have successfully fought and won in competition, it is not a Sport Ju Jutsu style. My vision for Mizu Ryu Ju Jutsu, was to reformulate what my own studies and research led me to believe was closer to the true essence of Ju Jutsu. Part real self-defence, part competition, part mental & emotional training, part creating a sense of community and part providing a safe environment for students to learn how to teach. Many traditionalists don't compete. Many Competition fighters have no traditional background. Many of both have no real fight experience…….We have all three! The experiences I have had through nearly 50 years of training, 3 decades of real fights and competitions, different rules or no rules, mean our syllabus is tried, tested and ever evolving.

The significance of the Mizu Ryu Ju Jutsu belt grade colours, their *kanji* and their associated meanings in this publication, are unique to this system of Mizu Ryu Ju Jutsu. Constructed when designing our syllabus which 'went live' April 24th 1994, our belt significations are influenced by The 7 Virtues of Budō, The 7 Liberal Arts and Sciences and other western esoteric teaching. They are not taken from, nor attributed to, any other syllabus or style of Martial Art that I was aware of at the time of establishing our syllabus. As such, although different fields of teaching may have a common lineage or focal point, please do not confuse or apply our information to the belt systems of other Martial Arts as they may differ significantly. Each art has their own reasons for the way their syllabus and grade recognitions are constructed, although I have been asked if others can copy ours over the years!

To use a metaphor I gave during an interview on Mick Tully's podcast a few years ago, Ju Jutsu is like milkshake. There are many different flavours of milkshake to choose from. Mizu Ryu, BJJ and Kito Ryu are some of the individual flavours of the milkshake, that we call Ju Jutsu. Once you've found the flavour you prefer, remember it is made of several different ingredients. Even the same flavour can have variations unique to each School or establishment. Banana milkshake from Burger King, may taste very different to Banana milkshake from Marks and Spencer *(other brands are available!)*. Whilst it may share some of the same ingredients, or even the same name, it is a personalised construct of the institution it originates from and the chef who designed it. Each establishment mixes the ingredients in a slightly different way, for different reasons with varying individual results, so the same flavour can taste very different from one place to another. Once you've found the flavour and mix you prefer, take your time with it. Savour it. Take time to fully appreciate the mixture of ingredients and learn all that went into making it. Some rush to go and make their own version before they've uncovered ALL the ingredients. You can make your own, no problem, just don't expect it to taste the same if you don't fully understand what went into it.

I hope you have many enjoyable years of practicing Mizu Ryu Ju Jutsu and enjoy furthering your understanding of the syllabus. Continue your obligation as a Martial Artist to make a daily advancement in your knowledge, to better yourself, to better serve and protect your family and the community within which you live. Enjoy the milkshake!

Tony Bailey

History of Mizu Ryu Ju Jutsu

What's in a name?

The syllabus for Mizu Ryu Ju Jutsu was officially founded in Basingstoke, April 24th 1994. Although the techniques were brought together earlier than that, this is the date from which the style was formally consecrated. The name of the style, Mizu Ryu – The Water School, was chosen as it represented the founding principle behind the philosophy of the style. It highlights the desire to attain a fluency of thought and action in all aspects of life, not just in fighting or self-defence. Many Martial Arts schools have chosen their names for similar reasons over the years. Given there is a finite number of word combinations, there have been several 'Mizu Ryu' clubs in Japan and elsewhere: Mizu Ryu Judo, Mizu Ryu Karate etc…. all of which have been founded at different times, by different people and are independent of each other, with only a similar name being the connection. My early research uncovered that the name Judo, had been used in Japan to name a style of Ju Jutsu over 130 years before Kano invented Kodokan Judo, so it's not unusual to come across duplication.

I remember having to explain this, many years ago, to a rather arrogant student in Italy. He had contacted me to ask why I was using the name of his teacher's school, even though by his own admission, the school he was referring to, was founded some 6 years after mine was established! After having provided him with some historical facts, I calmly told him that what is more important is the founder, the specific syllabus and ethos behind the style they teach, as these are what differentiates one system from another. You can call a technique 'Banana 1' if you want, names don't dictate the effectiveness of the technique, or the school. Knowledge of where, when and how to use that technique is much more important than the name. The name is an easier means of identification within the school, or to convey some part of the ethos to the students who study there. Quite often, these names can mean completely different things to those who do not study under that particular school. In fact, several different schools in Japan use the same names for their techniques as other schools, yet the actual techniques can be completely different. For example, the throw Yama Arashi in Takeda Ryu Aikijujutsu looks very different to the Yama Arashi throw from Kodokan Judo and we have 2 techniques called Ude Gaeshi in our syllabus, one is an arm lock, the other is a sacrifice throw. Some names are literal translations of the physical action, like Ushiro Nage (Rear Throw) and others are less logical, such as the afore mentioned Yama Arashi (Mountain Storm).

Where it all began

I began my own Martial Arts training in 1976 at the Summit Judo Club, Basingstoke UK, under Sensei's Derek Brownett and Len Dunce. My father had been a very good Greco-Roman Wrestler in London, trained by the British Olympic team coach, Jack Ingle. Understanding the benefit of fight training, having survived a stabbing when rescuing a woman being mugged and living in very turbulent times of open and violent racism, my father decided it was necessary for my brothers and I to learn some form of self-defence. He was right, even as a child, I had to use my skills many times to survive and control physical assaults. I became successfully proactive in my own defence by a young age, which was just as well as the first time someone tried to stab me, was when I was just 14 years old. The blade was aimed, very close distance, to my solar plexus. It happened so fast, yet I was able to successfully defend and disarm the attacker. I vividly remember when I got home and got changed, seeing a red dot of blood on my chest where the tip of the blade had nicked my skin through my clothing, so, had I not been so quick and able, I definitely wouldn't be here today to share the story and learn from the experience. I received very good tuition at Summit Judo club and learned an older form of some of the techniques, more akin to Kano Ju Jutsu as well as club Judo. This, in conjunction with my other studies, saw me become very proficient at using it all in the street.

I diversified my training into Ju Jutsu, Karate, Kung Fu, Kickboxing, Aikido and weapons, but I still maintained a close connection with the Judo club and Sensei Len (sensei Derek has since passed) and still do today, some 47 years later. As a junior member, I was fascinated both by watching the Seniors train in their randori, as well as their study and application of the Judo Katas, which mostly came from different styles of Japanese Ju Jutsu. This gave me the desire to learn either Kito Ryu Ju Jutsu or Tenjin Shin'yo Ryu Ju Jutsu, as these were the founding parent arts of Kodokan Judo. After gaining my Black Belt in a modern form of Aikijujutsu, I continued with this as I couldn't find a Kito Ryu or Tenjin Shin'yo Ryu Ju Jutsu school anywhere. This is what led to me training in so many different art forms simultaneously as I figured, if I can't find the original system, I would study all the component parts and try putting them back together. Almost 40 years after starting, I finally found a reputable teacher for Tenjin Shin'yo Ryu Ju Jutsu in the UK. After years of hard training with my long-suffering good friend and student, Sal, I was tested for and honoured to be awarded my Shodan in Tenjin Shin'yo Ryu Ju Jutsu by Paul Masters, Menkyo Kaiden.

Establishing the syllabus

As well as my physical training, from the age of 14 – 17, I spent a great deal of time in libraries (before the internet!), researching as much as I could about the old schools, adding everything I learned about the technique ranges, pressure points, weapons, strategies, religions, philosophies, healing and other teachings, together with my practical training in different arts. I eventually penned a list of what I was looking for, what I believed to be what Ju Jutsu used to be and this list would, years later, become the core syllabus of Mizu Ryu Ju Jutsu. I used the most easily recognisable names of techniques I had learned through various Martial Arts, combining terms used in Judo, Aikido, Karate and Ju Jutsu, to create an index which could be cross referenced with other arts. The original list was scrawled on a rough piece of paper, now torn and disintegrated, but luckily, before it became unreadable, I typed it onto A4 paper and have included a transcription on the next page, with some of the other surviving lists. I regularly check my old notes and add new experiences and methods, when assessing revisions of the syllabus or teaching methods with my club instructors.

Testing the syllabus

After establishing the club, I began teaching my syllabus alongside another that I was teaching at that time, for a modern Aikijujutsu organisation. I eventually became a 4th Dan under this school and was given the title of Shihan for my teaching position. As well as being part of the Management committee, I held the post of teaching other international teachers when they would come to annual UK seminars as well as going to their respective countries. I became British Heavyweight Champion in the competition form of Ju Jutsu and went on to compete under the banner of this organisation, in several different fight systems and organisations, including, Judo, Combat Jitsu, Shootfighting, Karate, Kickboxing and MMA. This, together with working for many years as a nightclub Doorman, gave me the added experience to trial and adjust the techniques I used, in a real self-defence format. When someone has had a few pints, wants to show off to their friends, or is 'coked up to the eyeballs', they don't fight by Queensbury or dojo rules, and they don't comply to pain in the same way! Let's just say that, after working as a Doorman for a total of 32 years, I've had the misfortune, or opportunity, to use every Kihon technique in our syllabus. All these experiences have helped me to maintain both a sense of tradition in homage to the techniques and knowledge of our forebearers, as well as a sense of reality for our techniques, for having used them in real situations, under real attack.

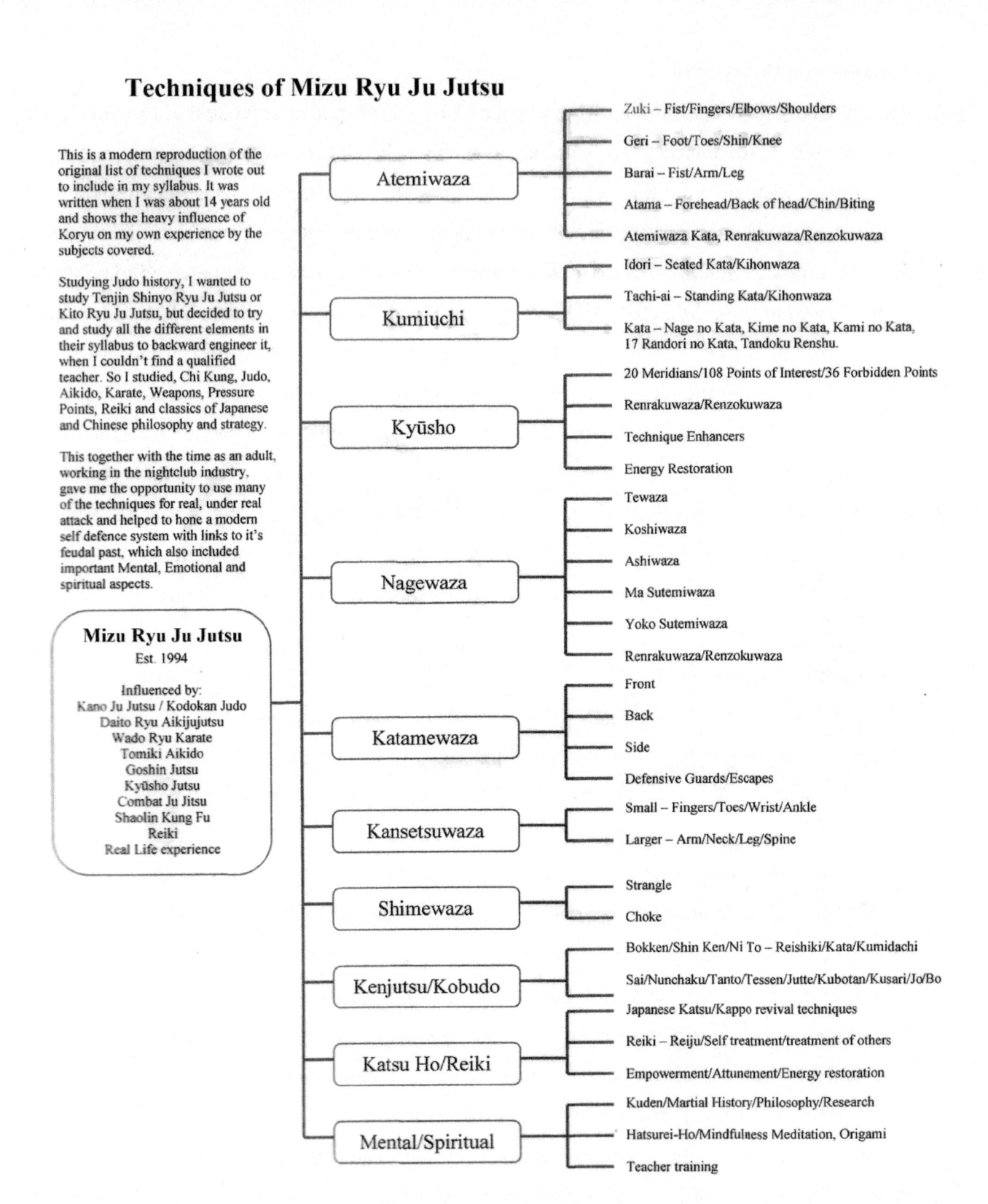

Techniques of Mizu Ryu Ju Jutsu

This is a modern reproduction of the original list of techniques I wrote out to include in my syllabus. It was written when I was about 14 years old and shows the heavy influence of Koryu on my own experience by the subjects covered.

Studying Judo history, I wanted to study Tenjin Shinyo Ryu Ju Jutsu or Kito Ryu Ju Jutsu, but decided to try and study all the different elements in their syllabus to backward engineer it, when I couldn't find a qualified teacher. So I studied, Chi Kung, Judo, Aikido, Karate, Weapons, Pressure Points, Reiki and classics of Japanese and Chinese philosophy and strategy.

This together with the time as an adult, working in the nightclub industry, gave me the opportunity to use many of the techniques for real, under real attack and helped to hone a modern self defence system with links to it's feudal past, which also included important Mental, Emotional and spiritual aspects.

Mizu Ryu Ju Jutsu
Est. 1994

Influenced by:
Kano Ju Jutsu / Kodokan Judo
Daito Ryu Aikijujutsu
Wado Ryu Karate
Tomiki Aikido
Goshin Jutsu
Kyūsho Jutsu
Combat Ju Jitsu
Shaolin Kung Fu
Reiki
Real Life experience

- **Atemiwaza**
  - Zuki – Fist/Fingers/Elbows/Shoulders
  - Geri – Foot/Toes/Shin/Knee
  - Barai – Fist/Arm/Leg
  - Atama – Forehead/Back of head/Chin/Biting
  - Atemiwaza Kata, Renrakuwaza/Renzokuwaza

- **Kumiuchi**
  - Idori – Seated Kata/Kihonwaza
  - Tachi-ai – Standing Kata/Kihonwaza
  - Kata – Nage no Kata, Kime no Kata, Kami no Kata, 17 Randori no Kata, Tandoku Renshu.

- **Kyūsho**
  - 20 Meridians/108 Points of Interest/36 Forbidden Points
  - Renrakuwaza/Renzokuwaza
  - Technique Enhancers
  - Energy Restoration

- **Nagewaza**
  - Tewaza
  - Koshiwaza
  - Ashiwaza
  - Ma Sutemiwaza
  - Yoko Sutemiwaza
  - Renrakuwaza/Renzokuwaza

- **Katamewaza**
  - Front
  - Back
  - Side
  - Defensive Guards/Escapes

- **Kansetsuwaza**
  - Small – Fingers/Toes/Wrist/Ankle
  - Larger – Arm/Neck/Leg/Spine

- **Shimewaza**
  - Strangle
  - Choke

- **Kenjutsu/Kobudo**
  - Bokken/Shin Ken/Ni To – Reishiki/Kata/Kumidachi
  - Sai/Nunchaku/Tanto/Tessen/Jutte/Kubotan/Kusari/Jo/Bo

- **Katsu Ho/Reiki**
  - Japanese Katsu/Kappo revival techniques
  - Reiki – Reiju/Self treatment/treatment of others
  - Empowerment/Attunement/Energy restoration

- **Mental/Spiritual**
  - Kuden/Martial History/Philosophy/Research
  - Hatsurei-Ho/Mindfulness Meditation, Origami
  - Teacher training

Wisdom + Strength = Beauty

I feel very strongly that the teaching we share with our students, should be balanced. It's important to me, that we don't teach only the violence, or only the peace. We must have a foot in each camp as this is what makes a more balanced individual and what I believe, is the highest-form definition of what makes a true Martial Artist. In furtherance to this, I also sought out knowledge of healing and mental and emotional training to balance myself. I knew a system such as Reiki had been used effectively in Japan but couldn't align myself with what I saw as the 're-invented' New Age form I came across. It just didn't feel right to me. I researched for a long time, until, almost by accident (there are no accidents!), I came across what seemed to me to be a more original form and much more in line with the mental, emotional and spiritual element I was looking for. I trained under Sue Norman, a fantastic teacher, who really helped me develop within this field and I stayed under her tutelage to reach RMT Degrees of Master Practitioner and Teacher. At the same time as finally embracing a more original form of this Japanese practice, I also began my journey into a serious study of Western Esotericism, through allegorical teachings, mentored by Ric Lovett. The first time I ever met Ric was me frisking him on entry to a club I was working at, on a bikers' night. Little did I know then, that years later, he would become such a good teacher and friend, that he would end up being Godfather to my daughters.

Both these knowledge and experience streams were steeped in work on the self through repetitive practice, mentored guidance and practiced application – exactly how Martial Arts is taught.

Speak softly and carry a big stick

We are taught that we need to be capable of violent action, as a last resort, to defend ourselves and others as life is precious and worth protecting. If we strike, we strike out of love, not anger. If we hesitate, we might miss our opportunity and allow an injury to take place which could have been avoided or stopped, so, we must act decisively. But, if we always act without thinking, we risk acting on impulse or allowing our emotions to override thoughtful action, so, when we act, we must also have considered options before we commit to action. Under the duress of a real fight situation, that's a very difficult balance to maintain. Some say impossible....

We can't very well ask someone to hold their punch whilst we consider all the options for defence. The time afforded to us to react to a punch being thrown is woefully small. This is why we need to be situationally aware. To understand, not just the answers to these actions, but to avoid dangerous situations in the first place and to recognise the physical and non-verbal cues which give us information about what is likely to happen. Zenshin. This is what gives us a little bit more time to choose how we react to a situation. Some physical techniques will be way in excess of what is necessary and proportionate to the perceived attack. Whilst we, by necessity of an unprovoked or surprise attack, need to act with a virtual flinch response type speed, we are still legally liable for excessive force, even if under the auspices of self-defence. So, knowledge of the law relating to self-defence and buying time to grade your response according to the level of attack, is something we talk about and practice a great deal in the club, because there are consequences to getting it wrong. Without this consideration, acting purely on impulse and without thought as to the consequences of our actions, we are no better than the thugs who commit the crimes in the first place. It is difficult, but not impossible. It is our right to defend ourselves, but it has to be necessary and proportionate. We do not want to become worse than the bullies. A great maxim which describes how we as martial artists go through life, is the West African proverb:

'Speak softly and carry a big stick'.

I have found that, knowing I can defend myself, gives me the confidence to look for peaceful alternatives, safe in the knowledge that, if all else fails, I will ably defend myself if necessary.

Self Defence

The legal test in the UK for whether a self-defence response is too much or not, could really be said to rest on the words necessary and proportionate. Defending yourself does not give you immunity from arrest, investigation or even going to court for that action. It's still an assault, even if for good reason. A Police Officer can investigate and make an arrest if they suspect a crime such as assault has been committed, even if you believe you created that assault as a legal defence of yourself, your property or in the defence of another person unable to defend themselves. There is evidence to preserve and statements to take as part of the investigation. What makes the difference in potential outcome, is being able to sufficiently convince the Police or a Court, for that matter, that your actions were both necessary and proportionate to the danger you perceived at the time.

You have to ensure that you do not go above that which was about to be or was being done to you at the time, so the minimum force required to adequately defend yourself and stop the assault. Once you have defended yourself and the assault on you stops, if you continue using techniques on that person, you would now be the one committing assault. As I say often in teaching and in articles: *'Perfect technique is useless without the knowledge of when to and when not to use it'*. I am not a trained lawyer and in all matters of legality, you should seek advice from a solicitor. I have, however, spent decades teaching this very same subject within the Security Industry as well as the corporate world and even at times, alongside the Police. I have lectured in college on the subject, written courses which gained national qualification status and have been called to act as a professional witness in court, so, my knowledge on the subject has been tested and accepted as trusted by the highest professional organisations.

Know your limits

You have to know when to stop. Some Judges will assume that as a Martial Artist, you should have more control over your actions. This is where sparring and pressure testing help so much. You have to be able to work with your emotions and mentally and physically be able to operate under the stress of attack. The more training you do, the better chance you have of making the right decision at the right time. But, even with the best training in the world, you won't know how you are going to react until you get in that situation. Situational awareness may help you avoid it altogether. If not, make sure you have tested your techniques as realistically as possible as, facing a real opponent in the street, with no Sensei, no referee and no rules, is not the best time to find out that your techniques don't actually work the way you thought they would!

Si vis pacem, para bellum

Unfortunately, the ability to defend or fight, is sometimes necessary to maintain peace and protect ourselves or others. A well-balanced mixture of physical skill, confidence, integrity and intent is needed to ensure we do the right things, at the right time, for the right reasons. We need to be making thoughtful decisions without falling foul to anger or negative ego. Anger is not the best mindset to use in conflict. Aggression has its place, but in any conflict, an assertive state of mind is better than an aggressive one. It's that whole thing of an athlete using aggression to win a race, whilst not being an aggressive person. Mental clarity allows us to fluidly seek strategies and make choices as changes become apparent. In this respect, the calm clarity we learn from the ability to be peaceful, helps us to become better fighters. Peace and conflict, Yin and Yang, two diametrically opposed opposites, with a little of one present in the other, working harmoniously to form a complete whole.

The mental and emotional intelligence training, together with the harsh, physical training, allows the adept to be in the middle of two different pillars of training. If they can get the balance correct, it creates an overarching spiritual mantle, keeping all the knowledge and application, wisdom and strength, in balance. Some of the most dangerous Martial Artists I have met in my time, are also some of the nicest people I know. These are true Martial Artists, who have the balance right, Gavin Mulholland 7th Dan Karate and Robbie Woodard 9th Dan Karate to mention but two. Lovely, lovely people with the ability, knowledge and intent on tap, to hurt you in the severest of ways. In fact, I describe Robbie, *(to his face)*, as 'A homicidal baby in the body of a giant with the biggest heart in the world!' He smiled and said 'I love you too'. These Martial Artists, and several more I have met in my teaching travels, personify that famous Latin phrase:

Si vis pacem, para bellum.

We all struggle on a daily basis, to maintain that balance within our physical, emotional, mental and spiritual training. Setbacks happen, but we remain ever connected to that desire for equilibrium and continue trying to make a daily advancement in our journey. I always tell my students that the study of Martial Arts is *'A spiritual journey of self-discovery, through physical means'*. Every day we wake up, we have different levels to our physical abilities and our emotional well-being. Very rarely do we get the physical, emotional, mental and spiritual all at the same level as each other, but we keep trying. That desire to achieve our goal, regardless of difficulties, helps us to foster a certain aspect of perseverance which is as unshakeable as *Fudo Myo-o* himself. Martial Arts is often referred to as the pursuit of excellence, but I would add more to that description:

'The study of Martial Arts is the constant pursuit of perfection. Even though we accept we may never reach it, it doesn't stop us trying.'

For more in-depth information, read the article – Martial Equilibrium p151.

Mizu Ryu Ju Jutsu Syllabus Requirements

Tying the belt

The obi - belt, in Japanese Martial Arts, has become even more important since the work done by Jigoro Kano - founder of Judo. He founded a new 'reward scheme' based on marking different levels of knowledge with several different belt colour grades. Within Koryu - old school Martial Arts, a belt was largely used only to hold the kimono jacket together. Knowledge levels are acknowledged by certificates or different teaching licences.

When tying the belt, there are a couple of different methods and knots used, but you'll find with a bit of practice, you'll soon get used to it. The knot must be at the front, in the middle of your body, roughly where the *Tanden* is situated as it underlines the importance of both the physical and energetic balance point at that location, more of which will be explained by your Sensei at the club.

Either 1) start with the centre of the belt at your middle and wrap both ends around your waist to your back. Change hands as the belt crosses your spine, and bring both ends to the front of the waist to tie the knot at the front *(this is more for non-grappling arts)*, **or**
2) start with holding one end at your middle and wrapping the belt around from one side to form neatly overlapping circles around the waist before tying the knot at the front.

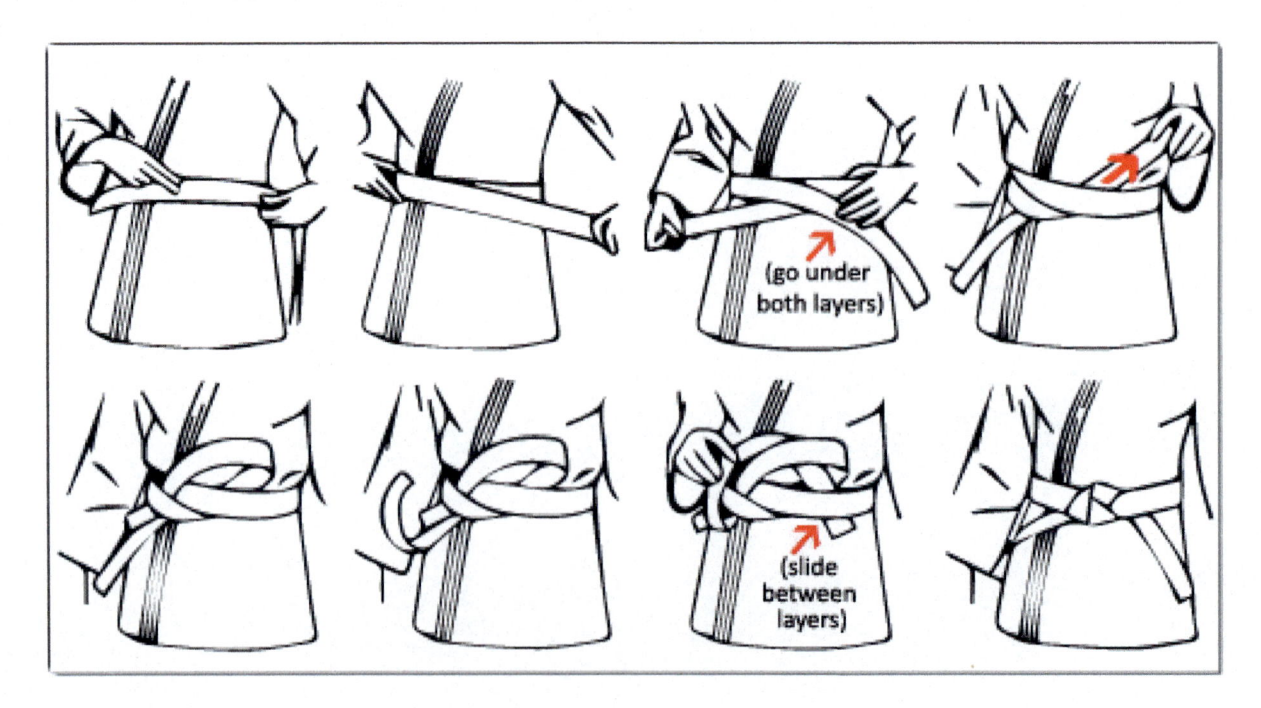

White Belt – Untested

As a White Belt beginner, you'll be introduced to a lot of new things, both physical and verbal. Don't worry, you'll use them so often that you'll soon get used to it. Once you've attained the correct standard, you'll be awarded Red Belt, the first belt of the syllabus. Use this part of the book as a reference whilst you're learning. It's your book. Make notes, drawings or highlight whatever you want to help you in your learning process. It doesn't matter how, as long as it makes sense to you, it's all good.

Mizu Ryu Ju Jutsu Emblem

You'll see this on our website and on our paperwork, it is the Emblem, or logo of our school. It was designed at the foundation of the school. Since then, whilst the overall design has remained the same, it has been updated with a better-quality graphic. The black Japanese kanji symbol in the middle is Mizu, which means Water. More detail can be found on p163.

Terminology

Ju Jutsu is a Japanese Martial Art, so some Japanese words are used in training. As I said before, they are used often, so don't worry, you'll get used to hearing and using them.

Japanese	**English**
Rei *(Ray)*	Bow / Respect
Sensei *(Sen Say)*	Teacher
Dojo *(Doe Joe)*	Training Hall
Tattami *(tat ta me)*	Mats
Matte *(Mat tay)*	Stop
Hajime *(Ha Jimmy)*	Begin
Gi *(Gee)*	Training uniform
Obi *(O bee)*	Belt
Hakama *(ha karma)*	Flared trousers

Kuden – Oral teaching (read through these for more detail at each grade)
Koi Carp & Perseverance
Mokuso level 1-3

Core Kihons

Throughout the syllabus are a set of core Kihons, which are learned, adapted and changed as you progress through the grades. Kihons are a set of predetermined question and answer techniques that you practice and demonstrate with a partner. They are used to guide learning the techniques and principles that form the foundation of your training. In addition, as the grades become split at Green Belt to factor in extra techniques and knowledge, an extra set of Kihons are learned at this level to add to the practical application in self-defence.

All core Kihons in our syllabus have been tested in real self-defence situations, under real violent attack or in competition. Understanding and applying the principles at the core of the technique is the key objective and keeping this core through all the grades, helps to guide growth in the *Shu, Ha, Ri* aspect of learning.

In addition, acting as an anchor to your beginning as a student, it sets a firm foundation on which to build the future you. As important as it is to be able to view and chart your progress and accomplishments, it is just as important that you not lose sight of where you started.

Senior Core Kihon names
1. Shomen Ate
2. Irimi Nage
3. Kote Gaeshi
4. Shiho Nage
5. Nikkyo
6. Mawashi Guruma
7. Waki Gatame
8. Sankyo
9. Haito Age Uchi
10. Hara Gatame
11. Ikkyo
12. Ude Gaeshi
13. Kuchiki Taoshi
14. Ashi Dori

Junior Core Kihon names
1. Yin/Yang
2. Gassho
3. Crane
4. Duck
5. Slam the Door
6. Leg pick up

Headlock Kihon Escapes

Side Headlock
1. Te Guruma
2. Sankyo
3. Yoko Guruma
4. Sukui Nage
5. Hiki Otoshi (Kami)

Standing Guillotine
1. Tani Otoshi
2. Sankyo
3. Yoko Otoshi
4. Jigotai (Head across belly)
5. Hiki Otoshi

At 9th Kyu Red Belt, you begin to learn the basic Kihon from a static position. The application of the Kihons changes as the difficulty of the grades increase. Additional techniques are added to the core Kihons, to maintain efficacy and graded response.

9th Kyu Red Belt

礼

Rei - Respect

9th Kyu - Red Belt represents *Rei* – Respect, of the 7 Virtues of Budo. This is regarding the politeness and respect shown not just at the club, but in all social situations.

The Kanji character actually means rite or ceremony but in a broader sense it means respect. It is often translated as morality, but as morality has other connotations, respect is a better translation.

The colour of the red belt signifies blood and the heat of the Sun.
It represents the blood of birth and the danger of the hot sun on the new-born which must be shaded, nurtured and introduced slowly to the dangerous Sun as, like knowledge, too much, too soon can be dangerous.

In terms of the 7 Liberal Arts and Sciences, the Red Belt represents Grammar – Correct language, the foundation and first subject learned in the Trivium.

Without a firm foundation on which to build, a structure has no stability. You cannot learn or apply complicated techniques without knowledge and understanding of the basics.

Thus, the first belt tested for, the most important foundation of the system, is the red belt, setting a firm base from which to develop both on a technical and personal level.

9th Kyu Red Belt

Ukemi
Mae, Yoko & Ushiro Mawari Ukemi - Front, Side & Backward rolls
Mae, Yoko & Ushiro Ukemi - Front, Side & Backward breakfalls

Terminology
Migi – Right | Hidari – Left
Hai – Yes | Iie – No
Onegaishimasu – Please, train with/treat me well
Dozo – Please, go ahead (Replying/offering)
Domo/Domo Arigato/ Domo Arigato Gozaimashita – Thanks, Thank you, Thank you very much
Ichi, Ni, San, Shi, Go, Roku, Shichi, Hachi, Ku, Ju – 1, 2, 3, 4, 5, 6, 7, 8, 9, 10
Mae, Yoko, Ushiro, Ura – Front, Side, Rear, Reverse.

Kamae
Seiza, Kiza, Hiraza – Quiet kneeling, attentive kneeling, active kneeling posture
Agura / Anza – Sitting cross legged
Ritsurei – Standing bow | Shizentai – Centre Stance
Zenkutsu Dachi, Kokutsu Dachi & Shiko Dachi – Front stance, Rear stance & Horse stance
Jigotai – Using Shiko Dachi as a defensive posture
Gassho – Prayer position for the hands

Atemiwaza
Shodan Kata

Baraiwaza
Jodan (Age Uke), Chudan (Soto Uke & Uchi Uke) & Gedan Barai – Upper, Mid & Lower Blocking strikes

Nagewaza
Tai Otoshi – Body drop
O Soto Gari – Major outer leg sweep

Osaekomiwaza
Kesa Gatame – Scarf hold

Kihonwaza
Snr – 14 x Senior Core Kihons from Ai Hanmi, Chudan.
Jnr – 6 x Junior Core Kihons from Ryote Dori

Kuden
Happo no Kuzushi & Triangle Theory
Basic Understanding of Self Defence Law
Mokuso level 4

Personal Development
Students must give a short paragraph on why they started the study of Martial Arts and what they have gained from it in their first 3 months. They must read it to the Examiner on the day of the test.

8th Kyu Yellow Belt

勇

Yū - Courage

8th Kyu - Yellow Belt represents *Yū* – Courage; the willingness to confront fear. Physical courage is the willingness to confront pain or risk of death and moral courage is the willingness to do what is right even under opposition, exemplified by integrity.

The Kanji has the important character at the bottom for *Chikara* – Strength. Sometimes written as 2 characters for *Yūki*, the second character of *Ki* – energy, if used translates the whole as Courageous Energy – Bravery.

A yellow belt spends much time pushing boundaries and putting in hard work now, to reap rewards of those efforts later.

The colour of the yellow belt, signifies the first beams of sunlight which shine upon the seed giving it new strength with the beginning of new life.
A yellow belt student is beginning to open their mind and begins to shine from within having observed the potential of what can be achieved.

In terms of the 7 Liberal Arts and Sciences, the yellow belt represents Logic, often overlooked for finding a more aesthetically pleasing or more complicated solution. It is about demonstrating reasoning and critical thinking. Drawing conclusions from principles, refuting false reasoning and beginning to understand strategic thinking.

The student must learn to see in as simplistic a form as possible, just as in the natural Zen outlook of a young child, so as not to build up unwarranted stress in anticipation, or to overcomplicate things, both of which are counter-productive in competition or self-defence, rapidly producing hesitation and loss of decisive action.

To quickly ascertain importance and act decisively, is a skill much needed in several different avenues of life, therefore showing an oft repeated theme that the microcosm of Martial Arts training, is mirrored in the macrocosm of life.

8th Kyu Yellow Belt

Ukemi
Tobi Ukemi – Jumping breakfalls
Tobi Mawari Ukemi – Jumping rolls

Terminology
Shomen/Sensei/Otagai ni rei – Bow to the Altar/Teacher/Class
Seito – student
Shihan/Soke/Shike or Shihanke – Master level Teacher/Grandmaster/Head of Branch Dojo
Senpai – Mentor | Kohai – Mentee
Deshi/ Uchi-deshi – apprentice of a teacher/ full time, live-in apprentice

Kamae
Hira no Kamae – Half kneeling posture
Chokuritsu – Upright stance
Ichimonji no Kamae – one line stance
Hira Ichimonji no Kamae – Kneeling one line posture
Neko Ashi – Cat Stance

Atemiwaza
Nidan Kata

Baraiwaza
Ashi Barai – Leg blocking strike
Atama Barai – Crown block
Kao Barai – Passive face block
Kubi Barai – Neck & face shield

Nagewaza
O Goshi – Major Hip Throw
O Uchi Gari – Major inner leg sweep

Osaekomiwaza
Kata Gatame – Single arm hold

Kihonwaza
Snr – 14 x Senior Core Kihons from Ryote Dori – End with simple throw.
Jnr – 6 x Junior Core Kihons from Ushiro Ryote Dori

Kuden
Yin & Yang Theory
Quadrant Theory
Mokuso level 5

Personal Development
Demonstrate a simple self-defence technique, describe the reasoning behind your choices and how this relates to UK Law on self-defence as you currently understand it.

Orange Belt

誠

Makoto - Honesty

7th Kyu - Orange Belt represents *Makoto* – Honesty. Honesty in words and actions. With definitions such as; trustworthiness, loyalty, fair, sincere, integrity, truthfulness, and straightforwardness, honesty is setting a firm foundation upon which to build a sound future.

Being honest not just with others, but with yourself by not over or underestimating your understanding, your ability to achieve, or your contribution to the lives of others.

The colour of the orange belt represents the growing power of the sun as it warms the earth and the seedling to prepare for new growth.
The orange belt is starting to feel their body and mind open and develop and basks in the warm light of the knowledge being passed to them, making progress on what has gone before.

In terms of the 7 Liberal Arts and Sciences, the orange belt represents Rhetoric – Confident expression. Communication and convincing the audience to act. In this way, we are starting to work on increasing practice of information delivery and therefore using a skill which will improve the students' confidence and their communication skills.

At this stage, the student becomes aware of being able to put some of the techniques together in a more practical sense, growing more confident in their own ability to use the techniques in a competitive and self-defence format.

This completes the Trivium, the first 3 subjects, laying a sound foundation for the more technical aspects to come.

7th Kyu Orange Belt

Ukemi
Sokuten - Cartwheel

Terminology
Tori – Attacker/Giver of technique
Uke – Defender/Receiver of technique
Keiko – Training / practice
Shiai – Contest
Randori – Free practice/sparring
Shinken Shobu / Jissen – Life or Death battle / Real-life application
Kuzushi – Breaking the balance
Hon – Original / True technique
Kazure / Henka – Variation of technique

Atemiwaza
Sandan Kata

Nagewaza
De Ashi Barai – Front foot sweel
Sukui Nage – Scoop Throw
Kazure O Goshi – Variation of major hip throw
O Soto Guruma – Major outer sweep of both legs
Ko Soto Gari – Minor outer reap
Ko Uchi Gari – Minor inner reap
O Soto Otoshi – Major outer drop

Osaekomiwaza
Yoko Shiho Gatame – Side hold
Kami Shiho Gatame – Upper four quarters hold

Kihonwaza
Snr – 14 x Senior Core Kihons defending Shomen Ate – Include a strike and a throw
Jnr – 6 x Junior Core Kihons from straight punch – including strike, throw & finish

Kuden
Superglue Theory
Philosophy of Mizu Ryu Ju Jutsu
Translation of Mizu Ryu Philosophy by Takase Shihan
Mokuso level 6

Personal Development
Demonstrate a simple defence to an attack, teach it to others, monitor them and offer help.

Green Belt

義

Gi - Integrity

6th & 5th Kyu - Green Belt represents *Gi* – Rectitude, morality, integrity – proper behaviour, to do the right thing.

The moral code of the Golden rule: -
'Treat others as you would have them treat you' has been used for centuries to define a good moral code. It can't be used for everything but should be used to govern the way you responsibly interact with others, now that you are gaining a more dangerous skill set.

Philosophically, it is perceiving others and yourself as one. This grade being an important milestone, the attributes of *Gi* join seamlessly with those of *Jin* in the next grade.

Green signifies the growth of the seed as it continues to sprout, reaching toward the sun and begins to grow more fully into a plant. A green belt student learns to strengthen and refine their techniques, to build on a firm foundation, solidifying roots and simultaneously reaching for new heights.

In terms of the 7 Liberal Arts and Sciences, the green belt represents Arithmetic, the first of the studies in the Quadrivium. It typifies the art of calculation and problem solving. A good exercise in logical thinking and seeking to understand why an answer is true.

Diligent practice is needed not just on the single techniques and their combinations, but on being aware of the counters and options available to an opponent based on what you are doing. Calculating these changes without being tied down by preconceived ideas is the next step towards reaching the goal of *Mu Shin* - No mind.

Having practiced more robust techniques, continuing to ensure there is no unnecessary or egotistical overreaction to an attack, forms an important aspect of understanding at this grade

M.H. McKee said: -
'Wisdom is knowing the right path to take. Integrity is taking it.'

Green Belt Supplemental Kihons

At Green Belt, an extra group of Kihons are added, in addition to the Core Kihons. These are practiced from the side headlock and standing guillotine attacks. Juniors are tested on 3 from the Side and 3 from the Guillotine, Seniors are tested on all 10.

Side Headlock

Immediately go to Shiko Dachi and control the wrist closest to your neck.
1. Te Guruma
2. Sankyo
3. Yoko Guruma
4. Sukui Nage
5. Hiki Otoshi (Kami)

Standing Guillotine

Post hand to hip to stop them creating lift and control the wrist closest to your neck.
1. Tani Otoshi
2. Sankyo
3. Yoko Otoshi
4. Jigotai (Head across belly)
5. Hiki Otoshi

Practice is needed to make flinch response defensive manoeuvres in order to set up the escape. A variety of strikes, finger breaks, biting and groin strikes are used with the escapes.

Guideline responses

1. Always immediately go to Shiko Dachi and control the wrist closest to your neck.
2. Post hand to hip to stop them moving in to create lift, if caught in standing guillotine.
3. If you must go to ground, posture up ASAP, no holds/locks, just get up and go.
4. Posture up – Use both hands against their face or arm or Doko point (TH17) to push them down. At the same time as pushing down, pull up your head hard & fast and straighten your back to break the grip.

6th Kyu Green Belt

Terminology
Kansetsuwaza – Locking techniques
Shimewaza – Choke & Strangulation techniques
Osaekomi/Katame/Gatame waza – Holding techniques
Newaza – Groundwork techniques
Atemiwaza – Striking techniques
Nagewaza – Throwing techniques
Maitta – Submit/tap out

Atemiwaza
Yondan Kata

Nagewaza
Ippon Seoi Nage – Shoulder throw
Seoi Otoshi – Dropped shoulder throw
Koshi Guruma – Hip wheel
Tomoe Nage – Stomach throw
Ushiro Goshi – Hip Counter
Yoko Otoshi – Side drop throw
Sasae Tsuri Komi Ashi – Lifting pulling sweep
Harai Tsuri Komi Ashi – Lifting pulling rear leg sweep

Osaekomiwaza
Mune Gatame – Back Hold

Kansetsuwaza – (Seniors/Jnr Brown Belts)
Ude Gatame – Straight armlock against the body
Ju Ji Gatame – Straight arm lock through the legs

Shimewaza – (Seniors/Jnr Brown Belts)
Hadaka Jime – Rear naked choke

Kihonwaza
Snr 10 x Core Kihons from Front & Side Headlock – Include a strike, a throw & finish
Jnr – 6 x Core Kihons from Front & Side Headlock – 3 x side headlock, 3 x standing guillotine

Kuden
Shu, Ha, Ri
Snr – Attend and pass Shoden Usui Ryoho & Western Reiki 1st Degree level course
Jnr – Level 7 Mokuso, Hatsurei-ho & Gokai Sansho

Personal Development
Demonstrate a technique, show and explain any basic biomechanical features, weaknesses, torque etc that serve as the underpinning knowledge behind the application of the technique.

5th Kyu Green Belt

Kata
Kami no Kata

Terminology
Te – Hand
Ashi – Leg
Hiza – Knee
Koshi/Goshi – Hip
Sutemi – Sacrifice
Tsuki/Zuki – Thrust/Punch
Keri/Geri – Kick
Atama, Kao, Kubi – Head, Face, Neck

Atemiwaza
Seiryoku zenyo kokumin taiiku – Tandoku Renshu

Nagewaza
Uki Waza – Corner sacrifice throw
Te Guruma – Hand wheel
Tani Otoshi – Valley drop
Okuri Ashi Barai – Sidewards double leg sweep
Tsuri Goshi – Lifting hip throw
Yoko Guruma – Side sacrifice wheel
Sumi Gaeshi (Judo and Aikido) – Corner throw

Osaekomiwaza
Tate Shiho Gatame – Mount position

Kansetsuwaza (Seniors/Jnr Brown Belts)
Hara Gatame – Stomach applied armlock
Waki Gatame – Armpit/Shoulder lock

Shimewaza (Seniors/Jnr Brown Belts)
Okuri Eri Jime – Sliding collar strangle
Sode Guruma Jime – Sleeve wheel strangle

Kihonwaza
Snr – 14 Senior Core Kihons from Mawashi Zuki – Include a strike, a throw & hold
Jnr – 6 x Junior Core Kihons from Mawashi Zuki – Include a strike, a throw & hold

Kuden
Snr – Lung & Large Intestine meridians
Jnr – Mokuso level 8

Blue Belt

仁

Jin - Benevolence

4th & 3rd Kyu - Blue Belt, probably the most important belt in the syllabus, represents Jin – Benevolence.
A desire to do good to others; goodwill; charitableness: to be filled with benevolence toward one's fellow creatures.

With great power comes an even greater responsibility.
We should hold the ideal to protect the weak and help the poor and distressed close to our hearts, in order to balance the harsh physicality of our studies with emotional kindness, thus fostering compassion to maintain the balance represented by In & Yo (Japanese), or Yin & Yang (Chinese).

Blue signifies the light of the blue sky, and the nourishment and fluency of water. The plant cannot grow without either.
A blue belt student should have mastered the early techniques and become more fluent with their usage and learns additional knowledge of the art in order to continue to grow and develop towards Black Belt level.
The student at this level, should now be moving more fluently within the techniques.

In terms of the 7 Liberal Arts and Sciences, the blue belt represents Geometry. The study of shapes, spatial relationships and proportions.

Knowing your position relative to your opponents' and where their limbs and balance are situated without having to look is a skill that should be acquired at this stage.
You will be learning to calculate probabilities, based on your acquired technical knowledge, as well as utilize other senses in this respect, which will help you begin to predict the possible responses of your opponent.

4th Kyu Blue Belt

Snr Kata
Te Hodoki – Tenjin Shin'yo Ryu
(studied for historical reasons only, not graded)

Nagewaza
Morote Seoi Nage – Half shoulder throw
Morote Gari – Double leg sweep
Ura Nage – Belly to side suplex
Tawara Gaeshi – Rice sack throw
Harai Goshi – Loin sweep
Uchi Mata – Inner thigh sweep
Yoko Wakare – Side separation
Ganseki Otoshi – Rock Drop (Ju Ji Grip, 1 knee)

Osaekomiwaza
Ushiro Kesa Gatame – Reversed Kesa Gatame
Makura Kesa Gatame – Pillowed scarf hold

Kansetsuwaza (Seniors/Jnr Brown Belts)
Ude Garami – Figure 4 armlock
Ura Ude Garami – Reversed figure 4 armlock
Te Gatame – Hand applied armlock

Shimewaza (Seniors/Jnr Brown Belts)
Tsuki Komi Jime – Push & pull collar strangle
Kata Ha Jime – Single collar strangle
Sangaku Jime – Triangle Choke

Kihonwaza
Snr – 14 x Senior Core Kihons from Mawashi Geri – Include a strike, a throw & finish
Jnr – 6 x Junior Core Kihons from Mawashi Geri – Include a strike, a throw & finish

Kuden
Philosophy of Mizu Ryu Ju Jutsu
Snr – Stomach & Spleen meridians

Personal Development
Demonstrate a technique, explaining the more intricate details relating to the balance points and body positioning, ranges and laws of motion, pressure points and angle of attack.

3rd Kyu Blue Belt

Snr Kata
10 Core Kihons of Spirit Combat Aikijujutsu – Forms 1 to 4
(studied for historical reasons only, not graded)

Nagewaza
Obi Tori Gaeshi – Belt throw
O Soto Makikomi – Winding throw
Ushiro Nage – Belly to back suplex
Yama Arashi (Kodokan) – Mountain Storm
Yama Arashi (Takeda Ryu) – Mountain Storm
Kanibasami – Crab Claw throw
Ashi Mochi – Leg scoop major inner sweep
Daki Age – High lift Body slam
Hiki Otoshi (Ju Jutsu, Judo & Aikido) – Pulling drop throw

Osaekomiwaza
Tenaguzaru Gatame – 'The Gibbon'
Ura and Yoko variations of all major holds
Escape from Kesa Gatame
Turn over opponent from top, front, side and control

Kansetsuwaza (Seniors/Jnr Brown Belts)
Hiza Gatame – Knee applied armlock
Ashi Gatame – Foot applied armlock

Shimewaza (Seniors/Jnr Brown Belts)
Nami Ju Ji Jime – Thumbs in strangle
Gyaku Ju Ji Jime – Thumbs out strangle
Kata Ju Ji Jime – One in & one out strangle
Ryote Jime – 2 handed lapel strangle
Do Jime – Body Scissor lock – constricting ribs / lungs

Kihonwaza
Snr – 14 x Senior Core Kihons from Mae Geri Chudan, Tobikomi Zuki
Jnr – 6 x Junior Core Kihons from Mae Geri Chudan, Tobikomi Zuki

Kuden
Snr – Heart & Small Intestine meridians
Masakatsu Agatsu
Mizu Shin

Brown Belt

忠義

Chūgi - Loyalty

2nd & 1st Kyu - Brown Belt represents Chūgi – Loyalty, to act faithfully.
The first kanji is Chū – to be sincere or loyal. It is made of 2 characters – the symbol for middle on top of the symbol for heart. Chū is understood as no conflict in the heart, faithful to what is felt in the heart.
The second kanji, seen before at Green Belt, is Gi – right action or duty.

Loyalty is thought of as devotion to a person, country, group, or cause.
Loyalty, not only to your Sensei, style and club, but also your own cause.

Sometimes, time, effort, doubt and failure are necessary transformative mediums allowing you to learn and see more clearly. So, through staying loyal to your training, you have learned to never give up on your dreams and follow through on your decisions, a key aspect of Nin – perseverance.

The brown belt colour, represents the ripening, maturing and harvesting process. A brown belt is an advanced student whose techniques are beginning to mature. They are starting to understand the fruits of their hard work as a beginner as they continue to grow towards the goal of reaching the Yudansha – Black Belt grades.

In terms of the 7 Liberal Arts and Sciences, the brown belt represents Music, which is applied maths and a fine art.
It also represents In & Yo, being opposing, yet harmonious forces of sound and silence. As such, the Brown Belt student should be able to demonstrate their techniques with a practical yet harmonious fluency, demonstrating an awareness of the balance between physical ability and moral rectitude.

2nd Kyu Brown Belt

Snr Kata
Shodan Idori – Tenjin Shin'yo Ryu Ju Jutsu
(studied for historical reasons only, not graded)

Nagewaza
Morote Seoi Nage – Half shoulder throw
Tsuri Komi Goshi – Plus Henka
Sode Tsuri Komi Goshi – Double sleeve throw
Kibisu Gaeshi – Ankle pick
O Guruma – Major leg wheel
Ashi Guruma – Lower leg wheel
Hiza Guruma – Knee wheel

Osaekomiwaza
Escape from all holds in the syllabus
4 x Control opponent from bottom and apply Shimewaza
4 x Control opponent from bottom and apply Kansetsuwaza
4 x Control opponent from bottom and reverse into Katamewaza

Kansetsuwaza
Ashi Garami – Figure 4 leg lock
Ashi Hishigi – Straight Achilles lock
Soto Ashi Hishigi – Heel hook

Shimewaza
Kata Te Jime – Single-handed lapel strangle
Jigoku Jime – Hell strangle / Crucifix Henka
Koshi Jime – Blocking hip strangle
Ura Ju Ji Jime – Clock/Baseball bat choke

Kihonwaza
Snr – 14 x defend against bottle attack – Core Kihons or own choice
Jnr – 6 x defend against bottle attack – Core Kihons or own choice

Randoriwaza
10mins continuous Tachiwaza defence against multiple opponents

Kuden
Snr – Bladder & Kidney meridians

1st Kyu Brown Belt

Snr Kata
Bokken Kumdachi, Kamae & Uchiwaza
10 Core Kihons of Spirit Combat Aikijujutsu – Forms 5, 6, 7
(studied for historical reasons only, not graded)

Nagewaza
Utsuri Goshi – Hip change throw
Hane Goshi – Springing hip throw
Hikikomi Gaeshi – Barrel roll throw
Yoko Tomoe Nage – Side stomach throw
Kata Guruma – Single line wheel
Hane Makigoshi – Lifting winding throw
Ude Gaeshi – Arm roll throw

Osaekomiwaza
Kubi Gatame
Teach 3 x different kaeshiwaza – escapes from a hold, into your own hold.

Kansetsuwaza
Tobi Ju Ji Gatame – Jumping straight armlock

Shimewaza
Tobi Sangaku Jime – Jumping triangle choke
Escape Hadaka Jime and apply Shimewaza

Kihonwaza
Snr – 14 x defend against 2 x attackers – Core Kihons or own choice
Jnr – 6 x defend against 2 x attackers – Core Kihons or own choice

Randoriwaza
15mins continuous Tachiwaza defence against multiple opponents

Kuden
Snr – Pericardium & Triple Burner meridians

Personal Development
This is tested against multiple opponents, simultaneously, in the timed randori part of the grading.

Black Belt

名誉

Meiyo - Honour

Kuro Obi - Black Belt represents Meiyo – Honour, good reputation, personal integrity befitting your family, teachers and peers. Let your words and actions bring honour to yourself, your teachers and your art.

According to Bushido, if one lost their honour, Seppuku was the most honourable solution, rather than bring shame on their family. The only way for an early Samurai to die more honourably was to be killed in a battle by a sword. So, it was most important to protect your honour.
In the early medieval period in Europe, a lord or lady's honour was the group of manors or lands he or she held title to. For a person to say "on my honour" was not just a promise of integrity and rank, but it meant he or she was willing to offer up estates as guarantee for their words and actions. A very costly mistake if found to be dishonourable.

Being an honourable Samurai could be seen as living daily by the 7 virtues and protecting them assiduously, as if your life or home depended on it, indeed, being ready and willing to fight and if necessary to die at a moments' notice to protect your honour. But, as we are not all ancient Samurai, but modern 21st century students of martial ways, we apply these virtues to our morals, in this sense:

Rei represents Respect,
Yū represents Courage,
Makoto represents Honesty
Gi represents Integrity,
Jin represents Benevolence,
Chūgi represents Loyalty,
Meiyo represents Honour

Just as in the Gokai of Reiki, it is important to try to live according to these virtues and remind yourself daily. Achieving your goal on one day is not as important as trying hard every day. As you know, a little practice every day is better than a lot of practice on only one day. So, do not be discouraged if you do not reach your goal, instead, persevere and commit to continue trying each day. Set realistic and achievable goals. Try only one day at a time. Try to live by the virtues for this day only. Then, tomorrow, try for that day only and so it continues. Do not worry too much about the future, it hasn't happened yet and is completely dependent on what you do today. Do not worry about the past, as it has already happened and there is nothing you can do to change it. You can, however, learn from the past, by making the most of today. Learn to concentrate on the now. This is what is meant by the Mindfulness that Buddhism teaches.

Every day in life is training, training for myself.
Though failure is possible. Living each moment, equal to everything, ready for anything.
I am alive. I am this moment.
My future is here and now.
For, if I cannot endure today, where and when will I?
A teaching I received from Soen Ozeki, Chief Abbott of Daitokuji Zen Temple, Kyoto. July 2001.

These are some of the most important lessons of traditional Japanese Martial Arts and as such are as indistinguishable from Japanese Buddhism today as they always have been.
Learn physically, be aware of your emotions, stimulate mentally and grow spiritually in all the Martial ways.

The colour Black here signifies the darkness beyond the Sun. If the Sun is common knowledge, the darkness is the knowledge beyond that which others can see. As you begin to teach others, planting and growing new seeds, you learn from them in a never-ending process of self-growth, knowledge, and enlightenment. Yudansha never stop learning and having now reached Shodan – 1st level or 1st Dan, you should continue to sharpen and define your techniques at a much deeper level working to achieve and maintain equilibrium of Mind, Body & Spirit.

In terms of the 7 Liberal Arts and Sciences, the black belt represents Astrology, being concerned with the vast universe and predicting the movement of celestial bodies. It is another branch of applied maths and a natural science, applying geometry to the physical world we interact with daily. Predicting the possible outcomes of your opponents' movements and therefore, strategically guiding them to movements that benefit your aims, is one aspect referred to as the 'chess' mindset of Ju Jutsu.

We can see that the understanding and prediction of things outside of ourselves helps us to prepare for the movements of our opponents by understanding how they think and feel from the choices we provide, but on a different level, is a skill leading to understanding of others on a greater scale more reminiscent of compassion that Buddhism speaks of so readily as we think of others and realize how our actions impact the lives of others.

Oneness, compassion born from a fighting art – that is the dichotomy at the heart of many true Martial Arts and something that a Black Belt should exemplify in their daily life.

Black Belt 1ˢᵗ Dan

Ability to demonstrate all kata and techniques from the whole syllabus, plus the following:

Snr Kata
10 Core Kihons of Spirit Combat Aikijujutsu – Form 8
(studied for historical reasons only, not graded)

Nagewaza
Nage no Kata – Kodokan Judo

Osaekomiwaza
Demonstrate 2 x submission techniques for every hold in the syllabus

Kihonwaza
Muto Dori 10 x defend against bokken/club attack – Core Kihons or own choice

Randoriwaza
30mins continuous Tachiwaza defence against multiple opponents
15mins continuous Newaza with different opponents every 5 mins.

Kuden
Jnr – Attend and pass Shoden Usui Reiki Ryoho & Western Reiki levels
Snr – Attend and pass Okuden Usui Reiki Ryoho & Western Reiki levels
Zenshin, Tsushin, Zanshin
Snr – Gall Bladder & Liver meridians

Acquired knowledge
Passing Black Belt means you have assimilated the techniques for several arts. Your grade is for Mizu Ryu Ju Jutsu, but your knowledge also reflects Judo, Karate, Kyusho Jutsu & Reiki. Shodan Tachiai – Tenjin Shin'yo Ryu Ju Jutsu and Kime no Kata – Kodokan Judo, is practiced at Black Belt 2ⁿᵈ Dan.

Personal Development
Write an essay looking back at your journey from the beginning in Mizu Ryu Ju Jutsu to now. Comment on what you have learned so far, if you have used any lessons in your everyday life, if you have noticed any personal changes during your study and how you feel about reaching Black Belt status.

Tony Sensei, is licensed to teach all levels, Shoden, Okuden & Shinpiden for Usui Reiki Ryoho & Western Reiki syllabus. To receive an official grade in the other arts, you would have to join the organisations and submit to their training/testing procedures. We study these arts, not to grade, but for historical reasons, to give thanks and to keep the knowledge alive. If you wish to professionally treat the public in the UK with Reiki, you must pass 2ⁿᵈ Degree Reiki (Okuden) to become a registered Practitioner and attain Professional Indemnity insurance. Reiki Federation membership is optional.

The Hakama

The Hakama is part of the Japanese attire covering the legs, looking like very large trousers. They have been worn as such for hundreds of years and there are several different types of hakama for different occasions. The two most commonly seen are the Andon Bakama – a formal type which has no divide and Umanori Hakama – most often seen in Martial training.

There are a total of 7 pleats in the Martial Arts Hakama, which refer to the 7 Virtues of Budo. The 5 pleats in the front are said to represent Yu, Jin, Gi, Rei and Makoto. The two pleats at the back represent Chūgi and Meiyo. Hakama for Aikido and Ju Jutsu are made slightly differently to those for Iaido and Kendo. Apart from being slightly stronger material, they also have longer ties, as the sword arts tie Hakama at the back (fig 5) and grappling arts tie theirs at the front.

Wearing Hakama for training

(For reference, this is the best google searched image for tying, but step 5 is more Iaido than Ju Jutsu)

Rules to wearing the Hakama are different for each art and dojo. **In Mizu Ryu Ju Jutsu, you have to be a Black Belt and a teacher to wear Hakama**. In Koryu Ju Jutsu, Hakama are worn by all grades on special occasions. Kendo and Iaido wear them all the time, regardless of grade or occasion and some Aikido dojo wear them only after Black Belt 3rd Dan.

There are several different ways of wearing the Hakama, especially when it comes to tying the knots. Formal occasions require formal hakama and formal knots. Essentially, Ju Jutsu has a rather pragmatic approach for training occasions, as long as it is secure, it doesn't matter. You can see this attitude in old photos of Japanese Masters' belt tying as well as hakama tying. Most follow the method set out on the previous page which is slightly different to the sword arts. All have the same viewpoint on the zubon (trousers), which is that they shouldn't be seen extending lower than the bottom of the hakama.

Folding the Hakama after training
Although different arts have different methods of wearing / tying the hakama, there seems to be one way of folding it after training which is used by the majority of arts. It takes time and practice when you first start, but as well as serving as a good Mokuso moment to collect your thoughts, it also saves you time and effort. Folding the hakama correctly at the end of training will help to keep the pleats in position and save you ironing it for every session. It's also a good way to practice respect, to look after your dogi/hakama, not simply bundle it in a bag. As a link to our Martial past, it is a privilege to wear hakama, treat it as such and it will last a lot longer.

Atemi Terminology
A few of the most often used terms for strikes

Punches
Seiken – Punching Fist
Jun Zuki – Front punch
Gyaku Zuki – Reverse Punch
Uraken - Backfist
Empi - Elbow
Haito - Ridgehand
Teisho – Palm heel
Nukite – Spear hand
Shuto – Knife hand
Tetsui – Hammerfist
Haishu – Back hand slap
Hiraken – Panther fist
Age Uchi – Uppercut
Mawashi Zuki – Hook punch
Tobikomizuki – Snap punch
Kakuto – Back of the wrist / Crane head
Yahazu – Arrow hand (ya = arrow shaft, hazu = nock, Yanone = arrowhead).
Ude Uchi – Forearm strike
Uke (Soto Uke/Uchi Uke) – Blocking strikes (Outer/inner)
Ippon ken – one knuckle / one finger strike

Kicks
Mae Geri Keage – Front Snap Kick
Mae Geri Kekomi – Front Thrusting Kick
Yoko Geri – Side Kick
Mawashi Geri – Roundhouse kick
Fumikomi – Stomping kick
Sokuto – Edge of foot
Ura Mawashi Geri – Hook Kick
Uchi Mikazuki Geri – Inner roundhouse kick
Hiza Geri – Knee strike
Ushiro Geri – Back Kick
Tobi Geri – Jumping kicks
Ura Ushiro Mawashi Geri – Spinning hook kick
Mikazuki Geri – Crescent Kick
Kin Geri – Groin Kick
Tsumasaki Geri – Toe Kick
Kakato (Otoshi) Geri – Axe Kick

Bokken Kenjutsu

There is a specific way to perform reishiki - bowing techniques for bokken, which is different to those of the live bladed swords. As we are not a Kenjutsu dojo, the techniques for reishiki and Kumdachi are basic and not performed with the same detail as Kenjutsu dojos, but they are to be performed with the same reverence and respect, nonetheless.

Bokken Reishiki

When not in use, the bokken is to be carried on the right side, with the right hand. When going from standing to kneeling, left knee first, followed by right. Right leg first to stand.

- Facing opponent, ritsurei, rest the kissaki on the mat and sit in seiza. Bokken still vertical on the right side, held by the right hand, cutting edge facing behind you.
- Bring left hand to the bottom of the bokken, both hands lift bokken to horizontal position. Thumbs roll cutting edge to face opponent as you bow to the sword.
- Place bokken on the tatami, horizontally in front of you, edge to opponent. Zarei twice – once to the dojo, once to your opponent.
- Right hand palm up, to tsuka, left palm down on Saya. Sweep left index and middle fingers to kissaki and draw bokken up to right side, edge still to opponent. Kiza.
- Chokuritsu. Ritsurei. Bring bokken, kissaki facing floor, to the middle. Back of left hand pulls Tsuka to left, step right foot forward and change grip to Chudan Kamae.

Bokken Kumidachi

There are 9 main kumidachi for bokken. Similar to other styles of Japanese Ju Jutsu and Kodokan Judo, the techniques are there to provide the student with a basic understanding of Kenjutsu and are from multiple sources. Practice of these basics will give you the opportunity to feel more comfortable with the sword, before trying to use it in practice with a partner.

The kumidachi all start with both Tori and Uke in Chudan Kamae

Kumidachi	Key Points
1 Chudan Tsuki	Otoshi Uchi, Men Uchi
2 Tenchin Giri	Gedan Kamae, Barai Uchi
3 Men Uchi	Mune, Men Uchi
4 Chudan Tsuki	Chudan Uke, Ichimonji Giri, Gyaku Kesa
5 Men Uchi	Otoshi Uchi, Chudan Mae Geri, Tsuka Jime
6 Ashi Giri	Nagashi Uchi, Mawashi Geri, Gyaku Kesa
7 Men Uchi	Otoshi Uchi, Hasso, Koncho, Kesa Giri
8 Tenchin Giri	Ura Nukitsuke, Mizu Kamae, Tsuka Ate, Kesa Giri
9 Tsuki	Hasso no Kamae, Ichimonji Giri

Kenjutsu Terminology

There are specific names used for stances, blocks and strikes, which can be unique to each sword school. Our techniques are only with a view to practicing a safe and proficient way to use the sword in kata and the names and techniques come from several different sources.

Some of the most often used terms are shown below.

Gedan Kamae	–	Sword Lower stance
Chudan Kamae	–	Sword Mid stance
Jodan Kamae	–	Sword Upper Stance
Hasso no Kamae	–	Sword Vertical Shoulder guard
Mizu no Kamae	–	Sword Upturned stance
Waki no Kamae	–	Sword Rear stance
Koncho no Kamae	–	Sword Cross gripped stance
Nuki	–	Drawing the sword
Chiburi	–	Shake off blood
Noto	–	Return to scabbard
Men Uchi	–	Head Cut
Kesa Giri	–	Diagonal cut
Tenchin Giri	–	Heaven to Earth cut
Ichimonji Giri	–	Horizontal cut
Gyaku Kesa Giri	–	Upturned rising cut
Tsuki	–	Thrusting stab
Chudan Uke	–	Centre line block
Barai Uchi	–	Diagonal block
Otoshi Uchi	–	Dropping Block
Nagashi Uchi	–	Swallow cut
Ma-ai	–	Fight distance between 2 combatants
Katana / To	–	Long sword, worn on left side
Wakizashi	–	Short sword worn through belt
Tanto	–	Dagger worn inside the kimono
No Dachi / O Dachi	–	Extra-long sword used at the battlefront
Tsuba	–	Hand guard
Tsuka	–	Handle
Kissaki	–	Tip of the blade
Saya	–	Scabbard

Technique application

Keiko

Keiko is what we normally call training or practice in the west. It's the time when we repeat, analyse and try to improve the techniques we learn. Improving our chances of making the technique work through repetition and attention to minor details, whilst building muscle memory, fluency and power. This takes the form of solo drills, partner work, Uchikomi (repetitive practice) and many other types of training to build on the different aspects like, speed, strength, accuracy, balance, intent and application. The practice is usually teacher led as the teacher is responsible for coaching the individual to work on their strengths and weaknesses, but keiko is also a time for the individual to identify their own areas of improvement, ask for advice and be self-motivated enough to work on their own improvements.

Kata

Kata are prearranged 'question and answer' drills, where there is a specific answer to an attack. These are learned and applied by everyone in the same way, in order to learn or practice a particular skill. The reason they are practiced the same way, with very little deviation or Henka or variation, is because the answer being practiced, is linked to an important aspect of that particular style or syllabus, that was realised by the founder. In this way, the students learn and apply the understanding that is key to the ethos and technically underpinning knowledge of the system they are learning.

Randori

This is known as 'free practice' otherwise known as sparring in the West. It is a time where we practice using the techniques in a semi competition style format, but without a time constraint, without a winner or loser. The key here is to learn to use the techniques with a partner, when neither of you know what you're about to do, to see how you can use your skill, intent, timing, strength and application to successfully apply the technique. This practice is always done with a willing and helpful attitude from both parties, but with a level of concentration that requires constant perseverance. In this way, it has some of the properties of a competitive nature, but the end goal is improvement of yourself and your technique through working with a partner, not winning a medal, trophy, belt or title.

Shiai

Shiai is a contest or competition, under a specific rule set usually against an unknown partner, but it can be with a regular training partner. The difference is within the rule set. Competition usually has more stringent rules than randori and is usually set within the boundary of a time limit. Different competitions have different rules, even within the same martial art. Each association sets their own competition rules and guidelines, and it is therefore important to understand the rules fully, before competing. Using competition rules within training at your own club can be an extension of randori and a way to check what your competition standard would be.

Shinken

Shinken Shobu, was originally a real sword to sword combat with lethal consequences. You can no doubt imagine, if two people faced each other to fight with real swords, only one person would be likely to be walking away from that encounter! For many years in feudal Japan, these types of duels were common. It was a way to not only settle major differences of opinion or arguments, but actually, a way to bolster your reputation with a view to gaining lucrative employment with a Daimyo or Lord, by becoming teacher to their own private army. Later, the term became used for any fight facing a serious challenge or risk, whether with, or without, weapons. As a link to this history, the other name for the Ju Jutsu influenced kata called Kime no Kata (Kodokan Judo), is Shinken Shobu no Kata.

Jissen

Jissen can be used at the front of a system or style name, to denote a real fight-oriented application of style – i.e. Jissen Karate, Jissen Ju Jutsu, Jissen Kobudo. Oftentimes, the techniques are less flowery and more direct than many of the techniques within the kata of such systems. Usually practiced with a partner to gain understanding of application, Jissen needs to be strictly controlled as the end result will lead to injury if correctly applied. It is important for true self defence knowledge, to practice Jissen, but it is equally important for the student practicing, to understand when to and when not to use that application, as spoken of in other lectures.

Senpai and Kōhai

Senpai 先輩 seniors and Kōhai 後輩 juniors, is a relationship with its origins not in Martial Arts, but rather in Japanese and Asian culture generally. It underlies Japanese interpersonal relationships in many contexts, such as business, school, and sports. It highlights different ranks of people in the same establishment, sometimes by age, but usually denoted by experience, knowledge and ability.

The senpai / kohai relationship has become part of the teaching process in Japanese Martial Arts schools. A senior student is senior to all students who either began training after them, or who they outrank. Age can also play a part in this as generally speaking, the Japanese foster automatic respect towards the older generation, but seniority in time served and grade, mostly outrank the age aspect in Martial Arts.

The role of the Senpai is crucial to the newer junior students. Senpai introduce or are responsible for, explaining / reminding Kohai about etiquette, work ethic, and other virtues important to the school.

Kohai are expected to treat their seniors with respect and this whole interplay of relationships plays an important role in giving the Senpai the opportunity to learn leadership skills. Senpai play a minor role as teacher to Kohai, leading by example and by providing guidance and encouragement. In this way, the Senpai / Kohai relationship and responsibilities is similar to the western concept of Mentor / Mentee.

So, to be titled Senpai is to be recognised and given a trusted position of importance. It is a minor position of power, not equal to the dojo Sensei, but the responsibilities show the Sensei's willingness to recognise the character and knowledge of the Senpai, to help guide Kohai in the training journey.

In some schools and businesses, the Senpai / Kohai relationship has been negatively exploited by unscrupulous Senpai, to gain unfair advantage and abuse their position of trust. There are stories of ordering Kohai to do unnecessary menial tasks to degrade the Kohai, harsh punishments for not reaching a particular standard, dealing out threats and violence and using the position to create immunity from reporting and other blackmail opportunities. It goes without saying, but I will say it anyway, this is not what the position should be about. Any such use, or misuse of the position, should result in immediate reporting, expulsion and prosecution, if warranted, of the individual concerned. In our club, our Welfare Officer is not the Chief Instructor. This is to ensure even the Chief Instructor can be in a position of scrutiny. It is to the Welfare Officer, that any such complaints about Senpai, or indeed anyone else inside or outside the club, should be reported. All such legitimate complaints will be investigated and not ignored. As part of the investigation, if the initial informal investigation warrants it, details will be forwarded to the appropriate authorities for a formal investigation.

Notes

Supplemental Information

Ceremonial Grades

Either side of the standard belt grades, are ceremonial grades with different significations and different requirements. Dan grades are signified by a band of gold embroidery around the end of the black belt and are dependent on both knowledge gained, and time served at each previous grade. Minimum eligibility is normally 1 year as a 1st Dan to test for 2nd Dan, 2 years as 2nd Dan to test for 3rd Dan, 3 years as 3rd Dan to test for 4th Dan, etc, up to the highest rank of 10th Dan. In addition to this there is an untested belt and 2 other ceremonial belts which consist of a combination of 2 separate grade colour belts, but as these are ceremonial belts, the syllabus truly contains only 7 different colour belts.

White Belt

The white belt or *Shiro obi*, is the ceremonial, non-graded belt of the untested beginner. It signifies Purity, a birth, or beginning, of a seed. In the western esoteric sense, white was used to signify purity and innocence. This was often depicted by the 'lamb of innocence' leading to clothing accessories for esoteric training being made from white lambskin.

A white belt student is a beginner searching for knowledge of the art. Looking for the right path to follow. The white belt represents the beginning of life's cycle, and the seed as it lies beneath the snow in the winter.

Black and Red Belt

At Black Belt 5th Dan, the adept can wear the ceremonial Black & Red Belt - *Utsuri obi*. The alternating panels of Black & Red symbolising perseverance, death & birth. Being at their peak with their physicality matching their technical knowledge, they are true warriors able to preserve life / create death if necessary.
The very epitome of power, responsibility and compassion that every martial artist should aspire to become through years of hard work and perseverance.

Red and White Belt

At Black Belt 6th Dan, the adept can wear *Kohaku obi* – the Red & White Belt. The alternating panels signify; white for the purity of intention and red for the intense desire to train with many sacrifices made over the years. *Utsuri obi* and *Kohaku obi* both represent perseverance and along with the White belt, are the most highly significant ceremonial grades in our syllabus.

Happo no Kuzushi

Kuzushi is the concept concerned with balance. Specifically, breaking your opponent's balance in order to simplify throwing or taking them to the ground. Happo no Kuzushi signifies the 8 directions in which the balance can be broken from a normal standing posture.

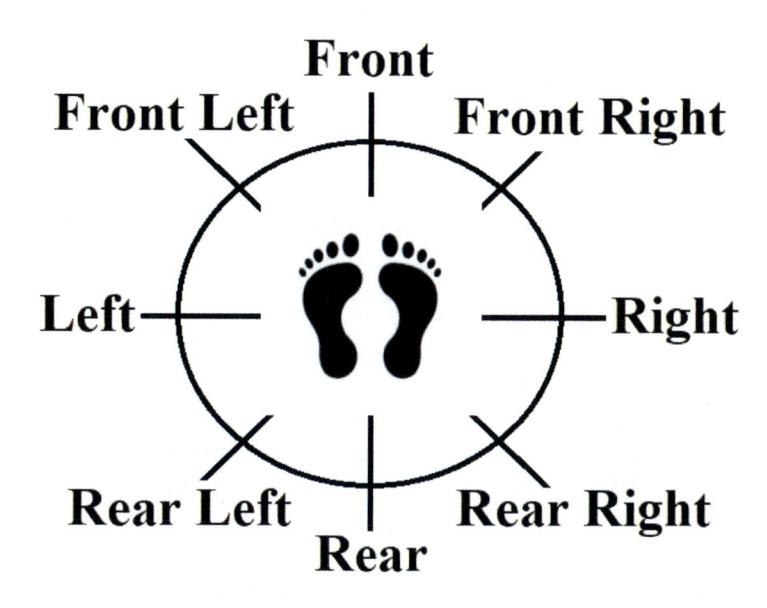

It is important to break the balance before throwing, in order to use less brute force and allow the technique to be successful. It is also important to realise how people react when their balance is broken and use this against them.

If you push an ordinary person away from you, their unconscious and automatic reaction will be to step forward, regaining the position from which you deposed them. If you pull someone towards you, they will step back for the same reason. Push them to the right, they will step back to the left and vice versa. Pull someone down on the vertical axis and they will attempt to straighten up. The same principle can be applied on the diagonal axis.

Training will help you to override these natural reactions in yourself, so that you may make a more informed judgement on directional change when needed. Understanding this and using it to your advantage against your opponent, will help you react quicker to your opponent's counter attacks, especially if they expect you to return to centre. We use Kuzushi in the 3-part process of throwing an opponent: *Kuzushi, Tsukuri, Kake* – Break the balance, enter for the throw whilst keeping the balance broken, complete the throw.

Training tip: Try to practice with a partner, using their energy. Using all 8 directions, try to exaggerate your partner's movements when they push or pull you, instead of re-centering yourself and fighting against them. When they push you to the rear, pull them towards you. When they pull you, you push. Practice this for all the 8 directions and observe the results of how quickly you can cause them to lose balance.

Triangle Theory

The Triangle Theory demonstrates the inherent weakness in stances and helps us to understand the application of technique in a particular direction, to maximise Kuzushi without expending too much of our own energy. Take the two feet of your opponent as two points of a triangle on the floor. The missing apex or third point on the floor, is where that person is most off balance to, should you push or pull them towards that missing third point.

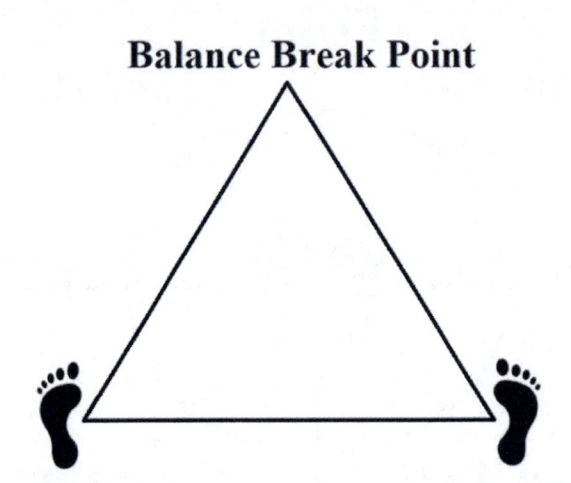

Balance Break Point

It does not matter which corners of the triangle the feet are placed, the third, missing point, front or rear, will always be the weak point in the stance. X marks the direction of the balance break point. Even if the stance is low and wide such as in some Shotokan Karate stances, the natural balance break point will still be the missing third point of the triangle on the floor.

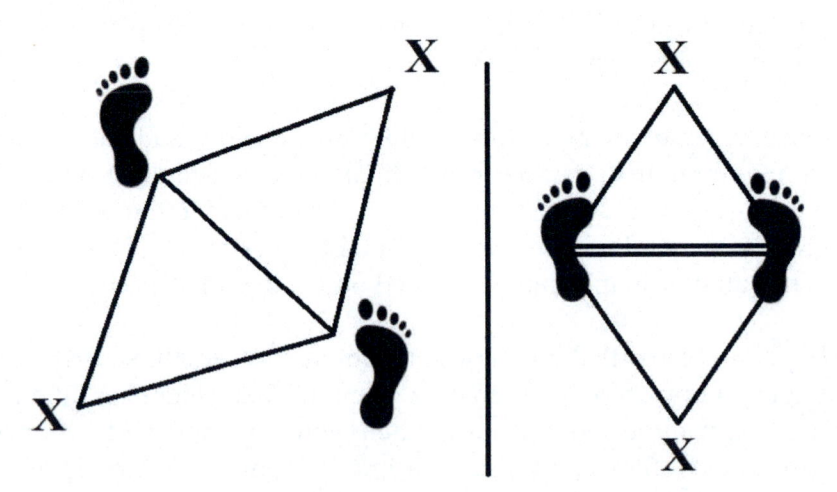

Training tip: Practice with a partner by taking it in turns to replicate the foot positions in the stances and push or pull your partner towards the X points. Find where and how easily the balance can be broken. Something to bear in mind. Some Karate Kata have strikes and counter attacks coming at a diagonal direction, to make use of this natural balance break point. When aiming through the X point, sometimes, you may need to change your direction or position, to make more efficient use of the angle of attack. Strike or throw through the X point of their stance for the path of least resistance.

Utilizing these tools helps us towards aligning with the concept of *Kuzushi, Tsukuri, Kake*.

Yielding

To bring this entry level Trivium on Balance to a close, let us look at something alluded to in the Happo no Kuzushi – Yielding.

To become effective in defence, you must learn to yield as well as learning to use direct pressure. Some will disagree and say it should all be about stamping your authority on the situation, taking command and forcefully pushing forward but, the truth is, sometimes a step back is better than a step forward.

Our brother and sister arts, Karate and Aikido, use both direct and yielding, but favour one more than the other. We should strive to attain balance of both within our art form.

In the previous 2 sections we covered how your opponent can lose balance easily if you pull when they push, yielding at its finest. It's a powerful tool and timing is key. Get it right, and it opens up all sorts of opportunities without wasting as much energy as force meeting force. In Japan, the Willow tree is synonymous with yielding:

Willow branches don't break under the weight of snow

柳の枝に雪折れなし

Yanagi no eda ni yukiore nashi.

Throw a stone into a heavy curtain, the curtain moves with the stone, absorbing its energy. The stone cannot break through the curtain, but drops harmlessly to the floor, exhausted of its energy.

Yielding is one of the ways in which a smaller person can throw a bigger person. Using their weight and momentum against them, redirecting, not stopping their movement. Not meeting force with force, helping it to be redirected or dissolved.

This is why we redirect more than we block. A block is a solid collision of 2 opposing forces. It means both people stop, and both have the same opportunity to strike again. Redirection keeps the attacker committed to their movement as you redirect that energy away from you and opens up counter strike opportunities for you. This is very much in keeping with Kano's maxim of *Seiryoku zenyo* - Minimum effort, maximum efficiency.

This concept can also be attributed to life outside the dojo in conflict resolution. Knowing when to push or when to hold back in a discussion, disagreement or argument, is one of the most often misunderstood aspects of communication. Good listening skills can help in so many situations. Just like the branches of the Willow tree, or the saying *'Water off a Duck's back'*, if we use good listening skills; recognising the stress, listening and giving space, empathising and not taking it personally; we don't try to own all that stress. It slips off, we return back to full strength and the person feels better having been listened to, not ignored.

So, yielding is as important in physical self-defence as it is in mental and emotional self-defence. Looking after yourself and improving communication between yourself and others, leads to less conflict and more chance of happiness and continued well-being.

Yin & Yang

The Yin & Yang symbol is synonymous with eastern philosophy, Traditional Chinese Medicine (TCM) and Martial Arts. The symbol represents Yin, dark, female and Yang, light, male - the universal law of opposites. Two diametrically opposed halves, both imperfect with a little of one in the other, coming together to create a harmonious whole. It is an allegory, alluding to the dualistic nature of all things and the fact that there must be a continual balance to maintain good order. This can be applied to the human form to either maintain or promote good health (acupuncture, herbal remedies and reiki etc.), or as a destructive force to be used to create ill health, injury or even death (many Martial techniques use acupuncture points to create injury).

In terms of Martial usage, we see Yin & Yang in virtually all techniques. We tend to create or promote imbalances by purposely manipulating these opposites:

- Left and Right
- Front and Back
- Top and Bottom
- Yin meridians and Yang meridians

In a very simplistic explanation, we disrupt the Yin & Yang by changing the natural order:

Take the left arm across to the right side
Turn the hand from prone (palm down), to supine (palm up)
Pull the head from centre to the feet

We can exacerbate this by using multiples of these angles and planes of movement:

Take the left shoulder down, towards the right foot (Left & right, top & bottom).

This creates a complex torque which we see used within Quadrant Theory.

Quadrant Theory

Quadrant Theory is the natural progression from having looked at Yin & Yang in terms of fields of movement. Here, we map and section the body into quarters during practice, and we pay attention to the difference when using the same technique in different quadrants.

Fields of quadrants
With our partner facing us, looking at them as a two-dimensional figure with height and width but no depth, we would draw a vertical line from the head through the body to the floor and a horizontal line through the middle of the body to form a cross. This gives us the quadrants 1, 2, 3 & 4 on the front facing field, as shown in the first part of the diagram.

If we add depth, taking into account the back of the person and therefore using 2 fields, front and back, with the same vertical and horizontal lines as before, we gain another 4 quarters at the rear of the person. From our front aspect, 5 is behind their right shoulder, 6 behind their left shoulder, 7 behind their right leg and 8 behind their left leg.

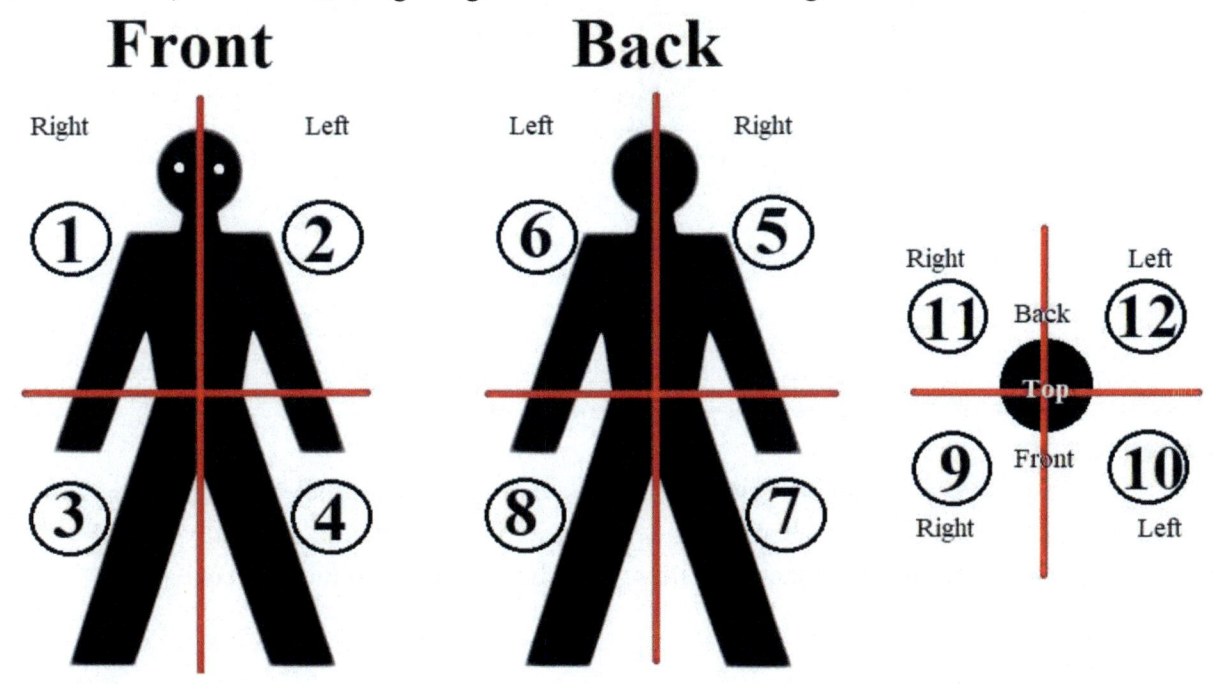

1 Field
Your opponent's right arm originates from quadrant 1. If it is taken down to the furthest away quadrant, quadrant 4, this creates an imbalance.

2 Fields
Taking that right arm, from quadrant 1 and direct it to the furthest away quadrant, quadrant 8. This creates more of an imbalance than using only 1 field.

3 Fields
A 3rd field can be created horizontally through the body, starting at the front and ending at the rear. This can create a diagonal plane of movement, which will generate even more of an imbalance. This highlights the reason why we are told to look for or create diagonals in the body, to make or take advantage of structural or biomechanical weaknesses.

Super Glue Theory

This is a very simple, but often forgotten or not applied technique enhancer.

There are a few main reasons as to why this is so important to apply when using techniques and it is relevant to all technique types, not just strikes. You will notice when it's missing because your techniques won't work in the way you were expecting, or at least, you won't feel as much in control and balanced as you should and the effect of your technique (force) is not felt as much by your opponent as it should have been.

I should point out I am **NOT** talking about using actual Superglue, it's just symbolic!

Close the gap
If you are close to your opponent, 'glued to them', when you move, they will too. If the gap between you both is too large, when you move, you will move into the gap and you will virtually stop at the point of contact with them, thus being unable to move them easily.

Surface contact
Increasing the surface contact will increase the sensitivity and control when executing the technique. When you are better connected to your opponent, you will feel the weight changes and movement they make in a much stronger way, if the contact between you is more secure.

Time on target
When you use a technique – a punch for example, after you throw the punch, if you take it off the target immediately, you will not allow all the momentum you built up, to leave your body and go into your opponent. Conversely, if you leave the punch on the target for a bit longer, that close contact allows the momentum you built up, to drive further into your opponent.

Three reasons why using the superglue theory (not literally!) will increase the chances of you getting a better outcome from your technique.

The 3 Laws of Motion

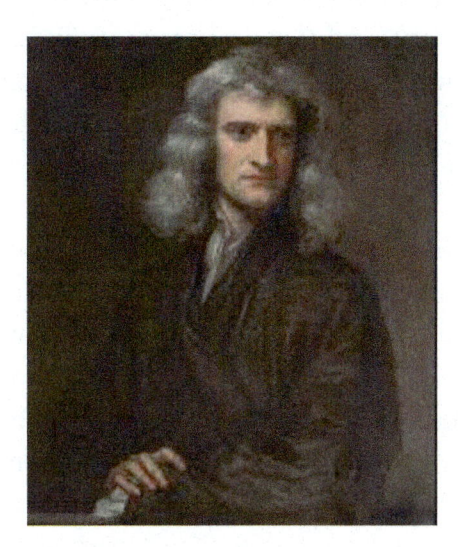

Sir Isaac Newton (1643 – 1727) wrote his theories around the Laws of Motion in 1686.
As the title says, there are 3 Laws of Motion.

In very basic terms, these Laws are:

1st Law = Inertia
An object stationary or in motion will continue that way, unless acted upon by another force.

2nd Law = Force
The equation F=ma is translated as Force = mass x acceleration. Force is created by a mass moving at speed. Increasing the mass and / or the speed, increases the Force.

3rd Law = Causality
For every action there is an equal and opposite reaction.

During your training, we will cover what these things mean in practical terms and how, using this information, you can increase the effectiveness of your Martial Arts techniques.

Mokuso - meditation

Mokuso is a fundamentally important aspect of Martial Arts training, for different reasons, at different stages of your martial journey. Ask someone what meditation is and they'll usually respond with sitting quietly and that's about it. In truth, it is about 'quietness', but that's only part of the story.

Mokuso means **'silent thinking'** but it is a double-edged sword of seemingly contradictory translation. It is a means of contemplation for silencing thoughts and silently thinking.

Mokuso is normally done at the beginning and at the end of a class. It can be done is several different ways, it doesn't always involve sitting, or being still and the reasons for doing it can be different according to the desired outcome.

At the beginning of a class
Mokuso is done as a practice for Mokunen – to set an intention, for two main reasons:

1. To section off or put aside the things that have happened during your day before you turned up to the dojo, so you don't bring negative or distracting thoughts onto the mat or allow them to interrupt your practice.
2. To set an intention for your practice. To focus on something you wish to achieve, work on and improve during your practice. Setting a goal you want to achieve by the end of the practice.

So, we see by **'silencing intrusive thoughts'** linked to our day's experiences and **'quietening the mind'** to achieve clarity of concentration, allows us to **'set an intention'** and concentrate on achieving a goal during our practice.

At the end of the class
The Mokuso at the end of the class is different to the reasons it is done at the start:

1. To contemplate the concepts or techniques covered in the practice, so as to order and cement those principles into a more permanent understanding. A kind of evaluation of your practice and how you can maintain that improved understanding going forward.
2. To figuratively leave the harshness and intent of the application of martial technique, in the dojo, not to take it out into the world. This is the necessary opposite to how we started and completing that Yin & Yang of our training.

So, just as in reiki practice, Mokuso & Mokunen is done at both the beginning and at the end.

Meditation postures
There are several ways to meditate which include different physical aspects such as sitting positions, hand postures etc. What is of upmost importance is the mental aspect of contemplation, regardless of position or posture. The classic Anza or cross-legged seated posture of Mokuso, is depicted by the Daibutsu statue in Kamakura (below).

Daibutsu holding Mida no jo-in mudra   *Hands holding Zenjo-in mudra*

Mudra, Mantra & Mandala
- Mudra are hand positions and are related to the original Indian practices which influenced the Mikkyo or esoteric Buddhist teachings in Japan. Each hand position symbolises something different, like those accompanying the mantras of the Kuji-kiri.
- Mantras are a short phrase or affirmation used with the intention of boosting self-esteem or confidence. They are used in esoteric teachings to invoke a kind of spiritual power. Some are literal, others, such as **Kotodama** (which we encounter at 2nd degree reiki) are deeper, short syllabic sounds, each with a specific frequency or resonance.
- Mandala are usually of symmetrical, geometric design, most often circular in nature. They usually represent a spiritual journey to reach enlightenment, but they can also depict specific icons, designs, concepts or goals.

The Daibutsu shows hands in Mida no jo-in, similar to the most recognisable meditation mudra, Zenjo-in. The right hand is placed on top of the left palm with the tips of the thumbs touching together lightly to form a circle. The Left hand represents the world of appearance (illusions) and the right represents enlightenment, thus representing the triumph of enlightenment over the world of illusion. This is sometimes seen reversed in Zen paintings.

Meditation techniques
Meditation in the contemplative term, is a good vehicle for the practice of mindfulness. In Mizu Ryu Ju Jutsu, we practice it in a variety of different ways, including seated mediation, walking meditation and producing origami. Sometimes that meditation will be in the guise of an end of class summary discussion, led by the instructor, on key aims and concepts from the lesson to take away from the practice.

Health benefits
Meditation has been proven to be effective not just in focussing the mind, but in the promotion of positive mental and emotional health. There are continuing scientific experiments into the benefit of meditation, which already clearly show the positive change in brainwave function, during meditation, due to its positive, stress reducing and calming effects. As such, regular meditation has been said to be beneficial for things such as stress relief, anxiety control, anger management, physical, emotional and mental health, problem solving, relaxation, rest & recuperation as well as others.

Meditation practice
Like any skill, meditation takes practice to get better at it and to benefit from the results. As well as practicing at the club, you can also practice at home in very simple and easy ways. Find a place where you can be undisturbed for the length of time you will practice for. Make sure this place is quiet and calm, with no distractions. If you find silence 'too loud', you can use headphones / earbuds, to listen to some low level, relaxing music whilst you meditate. Sit or lay comfortably. If you sit, make sure you can sit without having to adjust your position through the practice. Keep your back and head straight for better breathing, arms relaxed and use a cushion or sit with your legs, knees and feet in a comfortable position before you begin.

Start at small intervals of time and increase the duration the more you practice. The Junior levels, which they practice 3 times per week, are as follows:

Level 1 = 10 seconds
Level 2 = 20 seconds
Level 3 = 30 seconds
Level 4 = 1 minute,
Level 5 = 2 minutes
Level 6 = 3 minutes
Level 7 = 4 minutes
Level 8 = 5 minutes,
Level 9 = 6 minutes
Level 10 = 10 minutes.

Starting at small durations of time makes the practice achievable. Remember, like any other subject, we want to be setting goals for ourselves, but those goals must be achievable. After regular practice, you'll find it easier to get started and will recognise the benefits of practice.

Mandala

The Sanskrit word Mandala means circle. They can often be seen in Buddhist practices within a square border and are most often made with different coloured sand or paint. The lotus flower is often represented as, like the Koi, it represents triumph over adversity. The lotus flower starts life at the bottom of a pond, grows through murky waters towards the light and eventually is transformed into a beautiful flower when it reaches its destination.

There are mandala designs found in Hindu, Buddhist, Islamic, Jewish, Mayan, Aztec and Christian practices as well as others, and we can also see designs in nature, art and architecture. Generally, they tell a story, or represent a spiritual journey, starting from outside, working through different levels to reach the inner core, or goal, of enlightenment. Some are of very intricate designs that attempt to depict the universe, whilst others are of a simpler aesthetic design depicting religious or spiritual imagery.

Although originally of Eastern origin, in recent years the West has seen a massive increase in the practice of colouring mandala designs for creative and stress reduction reasons. Like other forms of relaxation and meditative practice, the act of colouring in mandala has been shown to help reduce stress and anxiety and to aid in focusing intent and setting affirmations.

At the end of this book, you'll find some blank mandala designs for you to colour in. Use coloured pencils, pens, crayons, paint, glue and glitter, whatever you want and make the colours as many or as few as you like. Whilst the design is often symmetrical, some asymmetrical colouring has also provided good results - there's no right or wrong way to colour them in, it is entirely of your choosing.

Make copies of the designs before you start, for future use as it may be interesting to look back on how differently you coloured in the same design at different times. Once finished, they provide artwork to adorn and enhance our environment, but the act of colouring them in, however, aids in our emotional, mental and spiritual well-being.

Reiki

What is Reiki?

Reiki is a system, which allows the healing or rebalancing of the body's vital energy to take place that our busy lifestyles would otherwise prevent or certainly delay.

Similar to Chinese *Qi Gong* or Japanese *Kiko*, this is done by the Practitioner connecting with the Ki (Chi) energy both within and around us to restore that balance. Reiki practitioners can then guide that energy to promote health and well-being in themselves or other people. In fact, when treating someone, it's much more like guiding them to the room containing what they need, opening the door and letting them take what they need.

This rebalancing can be for mental, physical, emotional or spiritual needs, but it is always thought that the body will take what it needs.

- It is not a religion, although it is based on certain esoteric practices of Buddhism, Shinto, Shugendo and Taoism.

- You do not have to be religious for it to work.
- The practitioner does not diagnose medical problems, they act as an intermediary between you and the energy you need in order to rebalance your energies.

- The practitioner does not use their own energy to heal you and can therefore treat many people in the same day without depleting their own energy reserves.

What does Reiki mean?

The 2 Kanji characters *Rei* and *Ki* can be translated as: *Rei* – Higher or Spiritual intelligence and Ki – Life force energy. In English it is often said to mean - 'Universal Life Energy' and is known in a longer translation as 'spiritually guided life force energy.

What are reiki degrees?

Reiki degrees are the levels of licence in recognition of knowledge acquired and application tested. They are similar to the Koryu martial grades before Kano proliferated the belt system.

- **Shoden – 1st Degree**
  Introduction, attunement and empowering you to work on yourself.

- **Okuden – 2nd Degree**
  Practitioner level, expanding on your own techniques and learning how to treat others

- **Shinpiden – 3rd & 4th Degree**
  3rd Degree Master level, more tools or 'Players' to increase your effectiveness as a Practitioner and further develop your intuitive skills. 4th Degree Teacher level, enabling you to attune and empower others to Reiki.

3rd & 4th Degree can be collectively known as RMT – Reiki Master /Teacher Degree.

The Founder of Reiki

Mikao Usui

15th Aug 1865 – 9th Mar 1926

- Tendai Buddhist
- Studied Kiko – Japanese Chi Kung
- Menkyo Kaiden – Yagyu Ryu
- Menkyo in Yagyu Shinkage Ryu & other Ju Jitsu systems
- Studied TCM (Traditional Chinese Medicine).
- Personally known to Ueshiba (Founder of Aikido) & Kano (Founder of Judo).

What can Reiki do for us?

Reiki has been known to have beneficial results for:

- Relaxation from stress, tension, anxiety and other related symptoms
- Sleeplessness
- Emotional turmoil and discord
- Feeling unable to cope
- Low spirits
- Depression
- Sports injuries
- Long term pain, such as back pain
- Rheumatism
- Arthritis
- Sciatica
- Low energy levels and M E.

How do I learn reiki?

Like Martial Arts, you are normally taught to learn and use reiki concepts either in seminars or regular weekly classes. Some people prefer to do whole day courses (2 days for RMT). This usually involves guided work completed by the student for several weeks in advance of the course as well as months of work in between the different levels.

I have taught both seminar style and regular class style and have found that, whilst there is no difference in the effectiveness or either, it's the same content, the regular classes spread the input over a shorter class time, but a longer calendar time period. This tends to give students more time to practice and ask questions of the teacher, before they are ready to move to the next level.

Like Martial Arts, there are many different styles of reiki and whilst the connection rituals for attuning or empowering someone can vary from one style to another, they all have the same goals and aspirations.

5 Elements in Martial Arts

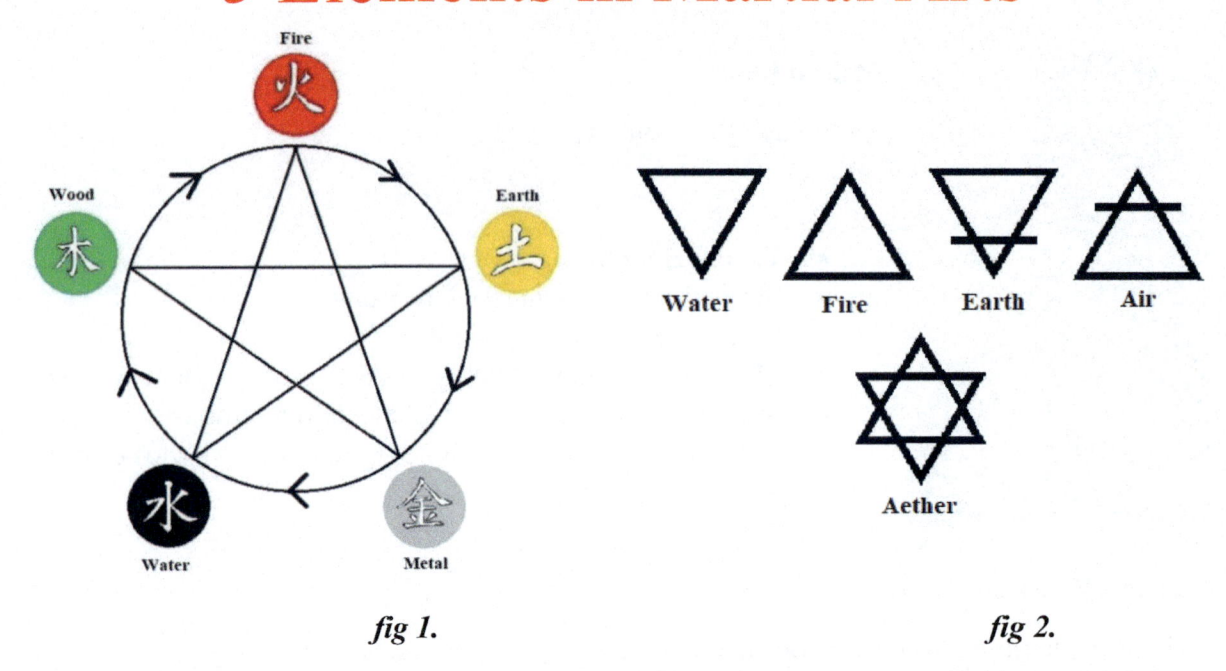

fig 1.   *fig 2.*

The Wu Xing symbol (fig 1) is representative of the 5-element theory of Chinese origin, which, when used in Traditional Chinese Medicine (TCM), predates Western medicine by thousands of years. In TCM, it charts the function and interconnectedness of internal organs and the energy which fuels them, by using a series of descriptive terms and prose to define those relationships. It is different to the symbols we see used in Western alchemy (fig 2).

In TCM, the internal organs are aligned to the 5 elements of Fire, Earth, Metal, Water and Wood. With each of the organs being labelled either Yin or Yang, it ensures there are both Yin and Yang for each of the 5 elements. Over thousands of years, the Chinese were able to discover and chart the flow of Chi or Ki *(Jap)* along meridian lines though the body, which were aligned to each of the internal organs. There are 12 main meridian lines in the body:

Element	Yin Meridian Lines	Yang Meridian Lines
FIRE	Heart & Pericardium	Small Intestine and Triple Heater
EARTH	Spleen	Stomach
METAL	Lung	Large Intestine
WATER	Kidney	Bladder (Urinary)
WOOD	Liver	Gall Bladder

There are other 'extra-ordinary' meridians. The 2 we use most often in Martial Arts are the Governor vessel and the conception vessel. The Governor vessel affects the energy to all meridian lines on the back of the body, the Conception vessel, all those on the front of the body. In Martial terms, the usage of these meridians and the various points on them for martial techniques, is known as **Kyusho Jutsu**.

Constructive Cycle

When used in the clockwise direction (fig 1), activation of these points is said to be on the constructive cycle. The constructive relationship is used to generate health, healing and harmony within the body. The constructive cycle is taught by way of a verse describing the effects of one element on the other. Loose English translation:

- *Fire creates earth (ash)*
- *Earth creates metal (ore)*
- *Metal creates Water (condensation)*
- *Water creates Wood (plants)*
- *Wood creates Fire (fuel)*

An acupuncture doctor, after assessing your health, will decide what has caused the root of the problem and treat that rather than just treating the symptoms. So, the doctor may find that, for instance, you have a deficiency of the element Earth in your system. Using his knowledge, one way he could address the deficiency, would be to stimulate Fire points and therefore generate more Earth element in the body.

Destructive Cycle

Martial Arts utilized this information to create injury or even death. It is the epitome of the dualistic nature of Martial Arts. If these lines of energy can be manipulated in a certain order to generate balance and health, then it necessarily follows that they can also be used in a different formation to cause imbalance and injury. The blueprint for striking and manipulating these meridian lines to cause injury and death, have been laying within the detail of Martial Arts techniques for centuries. The destructive cycle is taught by way of a verse describing the effects of one element on the other. Loose English translation:

- *Fire melts Metal*
- *Metal cuts wood*
- *Wood destroys Earth*
- *Earth destroys Water*
- *Water destroys Fire.*

Used in this way, the destructive cycle misses every other element as it perambulates the constructive cycle and in doing so, it traces the image of a **Pentacle Star within the circle**. This symbol would remind the student in which order to strike/manipulate certain points on an opponent, in order to create the most effective injury i.e. holding or striking a Fire point will promote a greater effect when holding or striking a Metal point.

Acupuncture or Kyusho?

Along each meridian line are several key points. The same points can be used for both Martial and healing application. The difference in outcome is from the angle, depth, direction and relationship with other points used, when activating those points. In other words, rather than thinking about a group of Kyusho points and a separate group of healing points, realise that there is just one group of points with different uses, depending on angle and application.

Points & Meridians in Martial Arts

There are 5 main 'rules' within Kyusho Jutsu which if followed, can make it easier to get more effectiveness from the techniques.

1. Attack many points on the same meridian
2. When affecting a point on one meridian, also use its Yin or Yang opposite
3. Attack points in the cycle of destruction
4. Attack by using a single 'extraordinary' point.
5. Use points according to the diurnal cycle

There are many of these 'Players to the game' or technique enhancers. The more technique enhancers you use, the more effective your technique. BUT you have to have a good, core technique to start with as without that solid foundation, additional enhancements are wasted.

1. Attack many points on the same meridian
Usually starting from the outermost point and working towards those which are closer to the center of the body, this method is an easy one to build into effective, defensive combinations.

2. Use corresponding Yin & Yang
Whichever meridian or point you use first, utilizing the paired Yin/Yang meridian within the same combination, is an easy enhancement to build into combinations.

3. Attack the points in the cycle of destruction
From wherever you start, make the next steps in the technique follow the destructive cycle for a much stronger overall effect.

4. Attack using a single 'extraordinary' point
Use just one point rather than a combination. A single point can be quite easy to use under the pressure of real time speed. Get to know the extraordinary points with great care. Remember, these are dangerous. But you can also use other, single points as well.

5. Use points according to the diurnal cycle
Diurnal is the opposite of nocturnal, but in the TCM world of Kyusho, they are referring to the order in which each of the meridians and their corresponding organs, are most highly active during the 24-hour day. Early TCM charted the order in which the organs are formed in the growing fetus. 1000's of years later, this has been proved correct by modern science. Related to the internal organs, each meridian becomes more active in a 2-hour window, following the order in which these organs were formulated. Martial application was said to be about understanding the relationship of one organ to the next in this chain reaction, rather than being strictly bound by the actual time of day.

Technique Enhancers

'Players to the Game' are like optional extras on a car. If the basic function works correctly, they are not absolutely necessary. On the other hand, if they make things easier, better, or safer, they are nice to have.

In Martial Arts, many refer to them only in terms of how they enhance Pressure Points, forgetting that Pressure Points as a single subject area, is just one of many 'players' that can be used to increase the effectiveness of the core technique being used. We have seen the '5 Rules' already, but there have been up to 200 technique enhancers listed over the years. Some of the main enhancers you will either use or hear about when using Kyusho, are listed below.

Footwork
Making sure that in a strike, your feet are pointing towards your opponent so as to work with the natural planes of movement for your joints, rather than against them. *(Think F=ma)*

Complex Torque
The body can resist one plane of movement easily, but we find it extremely difficult to resist more than one plane of movement at the same time. *(Think diagonals)*

Intent
In Kyusho and in Reiki, there is a saying 'Where Intention goes, energy flows' Your energy follows your intent. Your technique will become more powerful when you 'intend' it to. Whether you believe this is because you are more focused, or that it is something more mystical, is not important right now. Players of **Colour visualization** and **Sound** are similar. Science now backs many such ancient teachings like intent and *Kotodama* (syllabic sounds).

Use Figure 8's
Applying a technique in more than one direction, travelling the path of all the Quadrants in order. There are figure 8's vertically, horizontally and diagonally that are easy to apply.

The Microcosmic Orbit
The player **'Tongue to the roof of the mouth'** creates the microcosmic orbit, by placing the tongue to the roof of the mouth and using the pelvic floor muscles to contract the Huiyin point (CV-1). This internally connects the Governing and Conception vessels, and forms what is known as the Small Heavenly Circle, or the Microcosmic Orbit. This is used to enhance the available energy and power in both Martial Arts technique and in Reiki healing.

Bubbling Spring
This is where you activate the acupoint KI-1 by lifting your heal and pushing through that point. It is said to 'energise' the system, create more Ki flow and is similar to a resuscitation technique we use to counteract a strike to the groin.

All these and more, require more detailed study and careful application in practice.

Pressure Points in Kihons

This is not an exhaustive list, but it is enough to point out some of the key details to look at when practicing, so as to improve the accuracy and application of the Kihons and associated techniques.

The table shows some key areas to check when applying the Kihons to improve efficacy.

Kihon	Key Points
Shomen Ate	L8, H6, L8, TH4, CV23, LI18
Irimi Nage	H6, L8, GB20, S9
Kote Gaeshi	H6, L8, MUE13, TH3, SI6
Shiho Nage	L8, TH3
Nikkyo	LI4, SI5, LI11, L5
Mawashi Guruma	L2, GB25
Waki Gatame	H6, L8, S34, TH11, TH9
Sankyo	LI4, H8, P9
Haito Age Uchi	H6, L8, CV1
Hara Gatame	H6, L8, CV24, CV26
Ikkyo	SI6, LI5, TH10, TH11
Ude Gaeshi	H6, L8, TH3, L9
Kuchiki Taoshi	H6, L8, UB40
Ashi Dori	H6, L8, B61, S36

As the main meridians and the points on those meridians are bilateral, the points are mirrored across the centre of the body, therefore, available with the same potential result, regardless of whether the technique is applied left-handed or right-handed.

As Kyusho or Pressure Points are found all over the body, they can be found within the techniques of not just punching and kicking, but also throws, holds and submissions as well.

Diurnal Cycle

This diagram shows the 2-hour windows in which each meridian is more active and therefore, the relationship of meridians, one to the next in the Diurnal cycle.

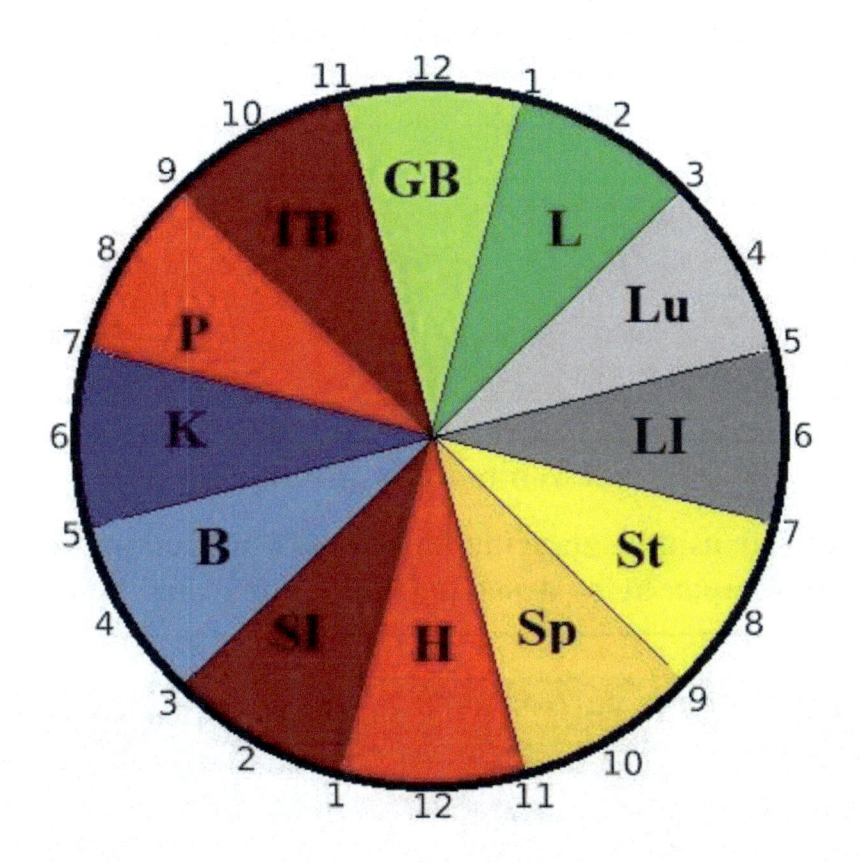

- 3 a.m. to 5 a.m.   Lung
- 5 a.m. to 7 a.m.   Large Intestine
- 7 a.m. to 9 a.m.   Stomach
- 9 a.m. to 11 a.m.   Spleen
- 11 a.m. to 1 a.m.   Heart
- 1 p.m. to 3 p.m.   Small Intestine
- 3 p.m. to 5 p.m.   Urinary Bladder
- 5 p.m. to 7 p.m.   Kidney
- 7 p.m. to 9 p.m.   Pericardium
- 9 p.m. to 11 p.m.   Triple Burner
- 11 p.m. to 1 a.m.   Gall Bladder
- 1 a.m. to 3 a.m.   Liver

From our perspective, it is more practical to consider the relationship of one organ being the gateway to the next in this order, rather than being specific to the actual time of activation. When someone grabs you, you don't ask them to hold still till 3am before using points!

Colour Visualisation as a player

As an additional 'visual' enhancement to the player of intent, try experimenting with the colour visualization player that I was introduced to when sharing knowledge with the UK arm of Dragon Society International (DSI). You have to really visualise the technique being saturated in and made of, the colour and associated action represented for it to work. It isn't some mystical or magical art, I understand it as just a different way to help you correctly apply intent in your technique, for those of us who are more visual in our thought processes.

> **Use Red for extra penetration with a strike**
>
> When punching visualise driving a big red-hot stake deep into your opponent with your fist.

> **Use White when cutting**
>
> If striking or using a glancing blow or sawing action, visualise the weapon being a searing white-hot sword blade

> **Use Black when absorbing**
>
> When receiving energy from your opponent, become a black hole or heavy black curtain and totally absorb the energy

> **Use Green when you want your opponent to go down**
>
> Visualise throwing your opponent down a big green slide, or a big green sink hole opening up underneath them

- Choose a technique that is simple to apply and easy to control
- Use the technique at low level, without the player
- Make sure your partner gives you a number from 0-10 as to the effect they felt
- Ensure you adjust your technique to produce a low-level number, not more than 5 or 6
- Using the same level of power, repeat it and add the colour visualization
- Was there a difference in the number level felt by your partner when you used colour?
- Try all of them and also chart your findings with any other colours

The 12 Main Meridians

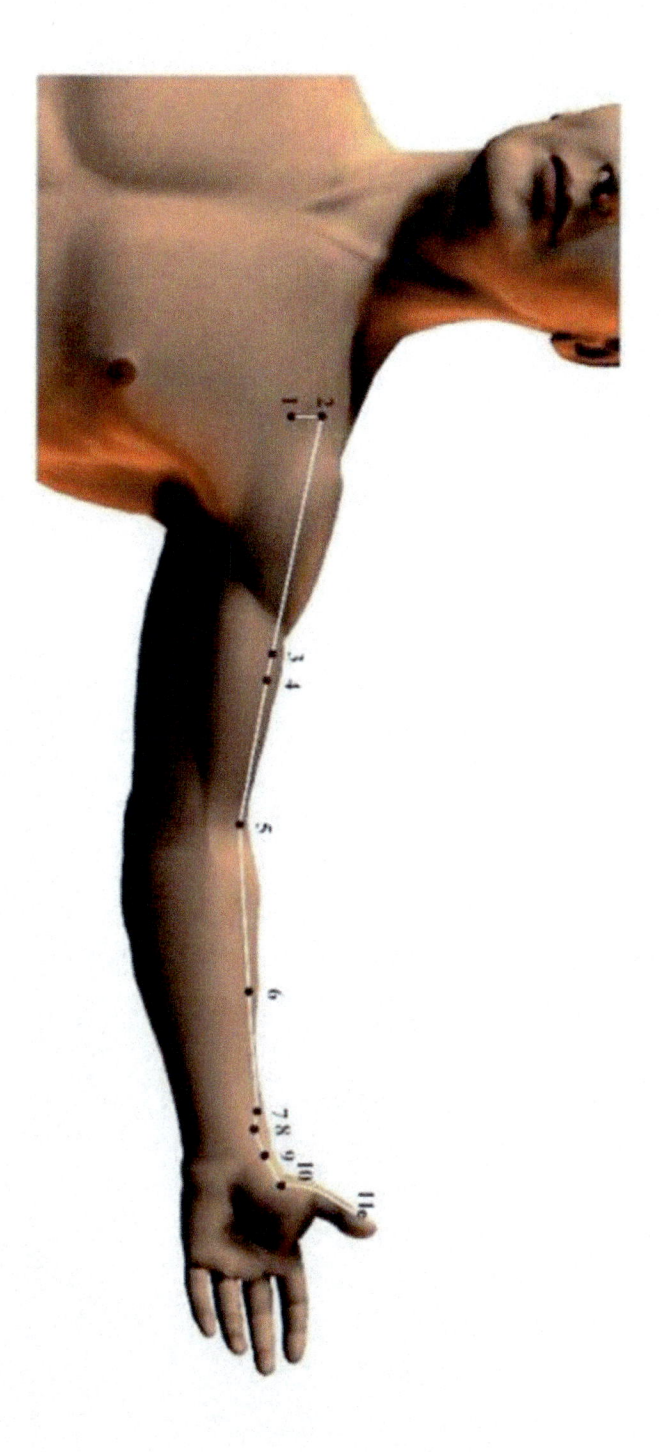

Lung Meridian

75

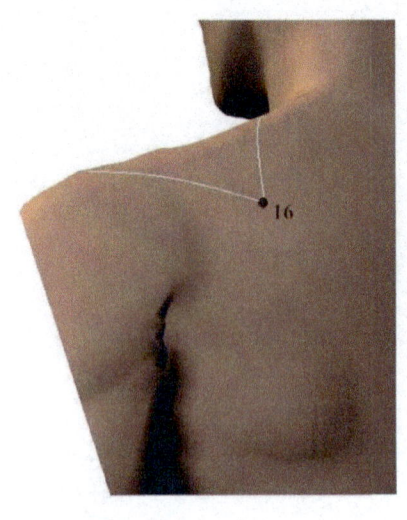

Lg Intestine Meridian

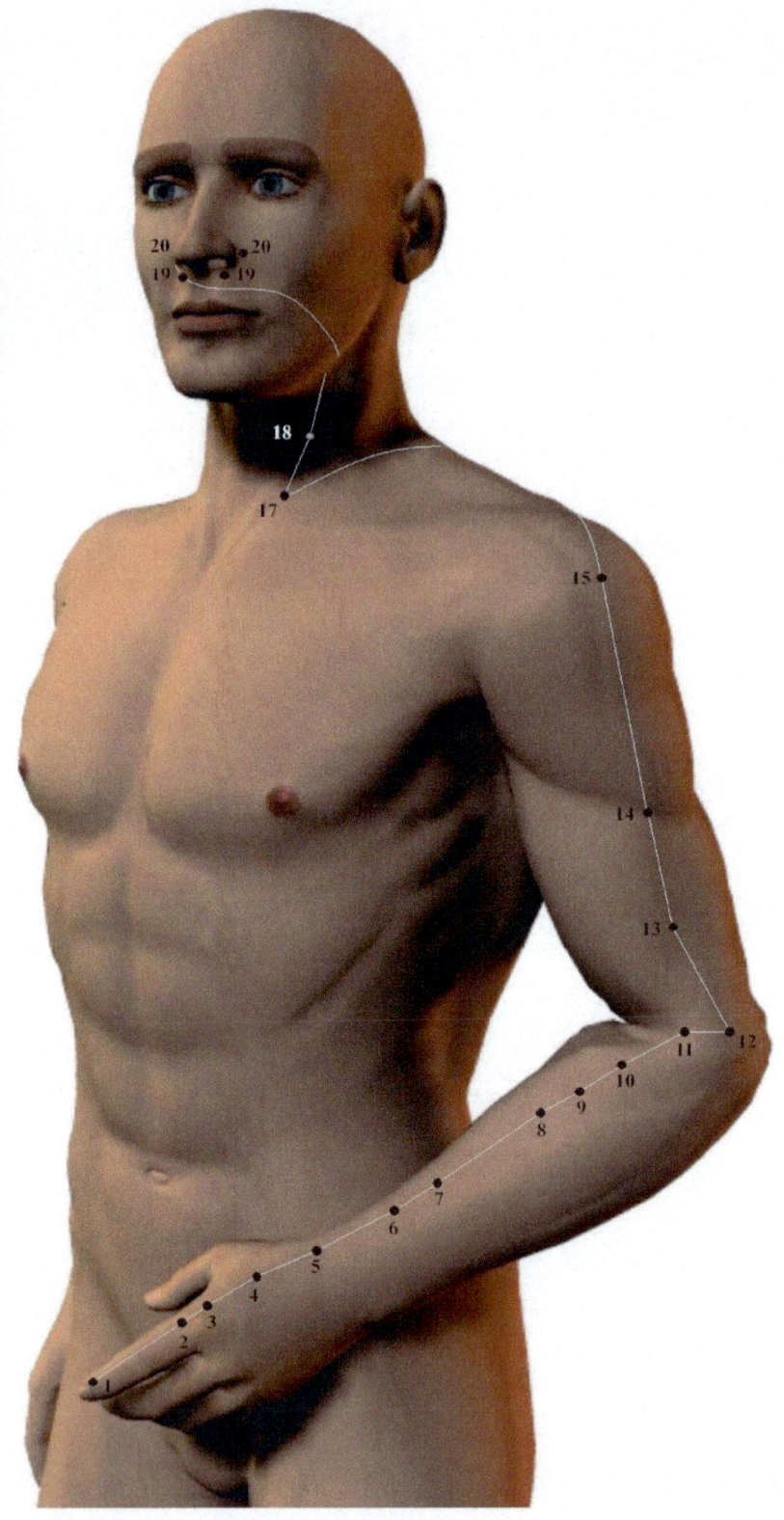

Stomach Meridian

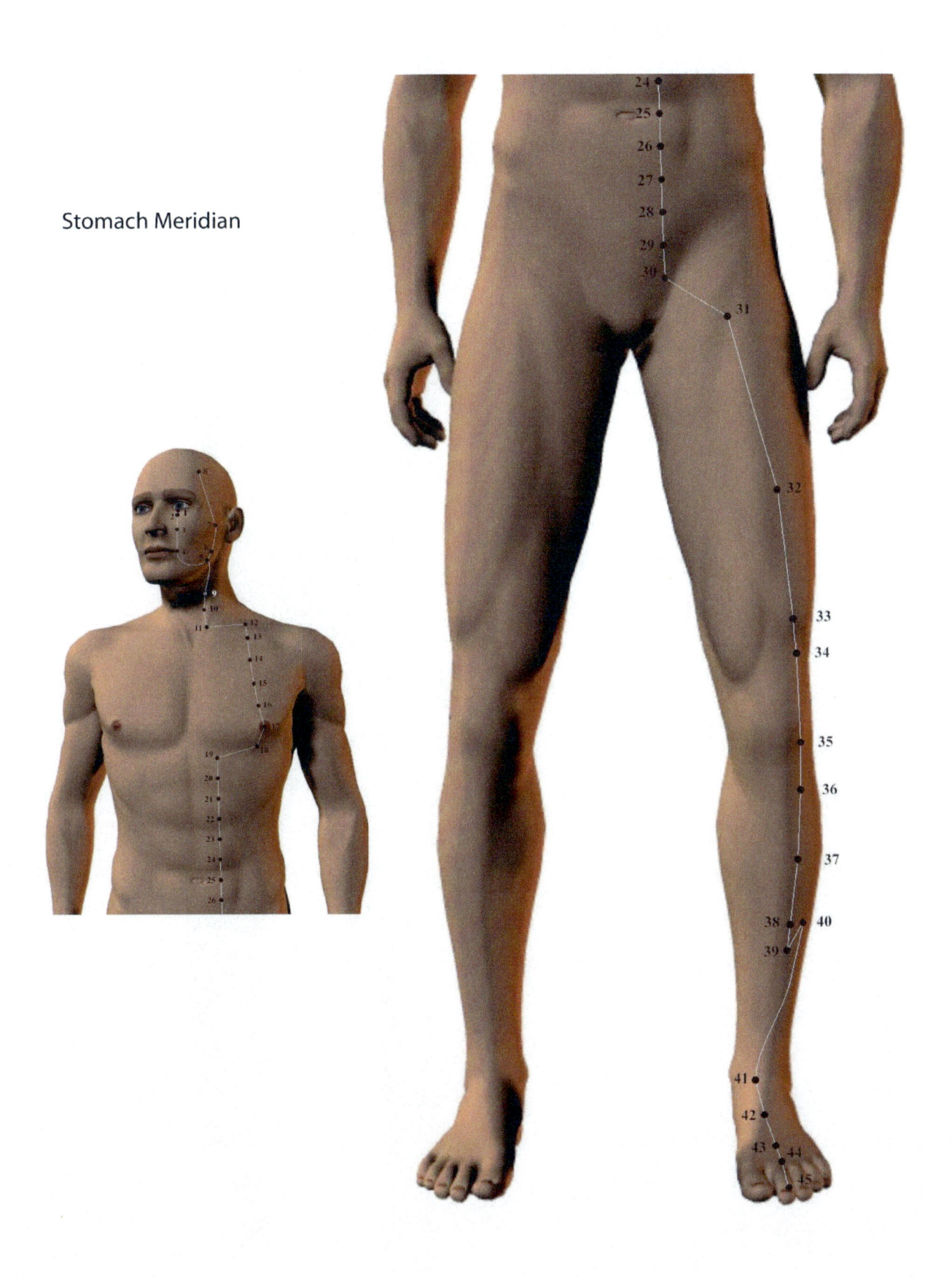

Spleen Meridian

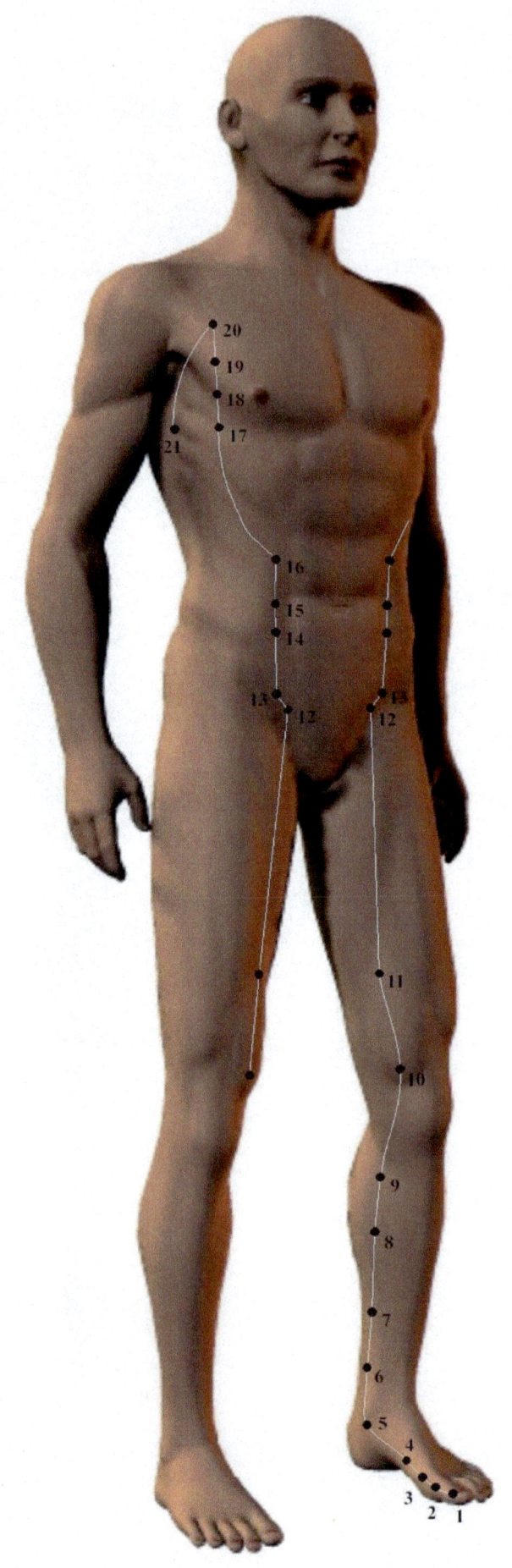

Sm Intenstine

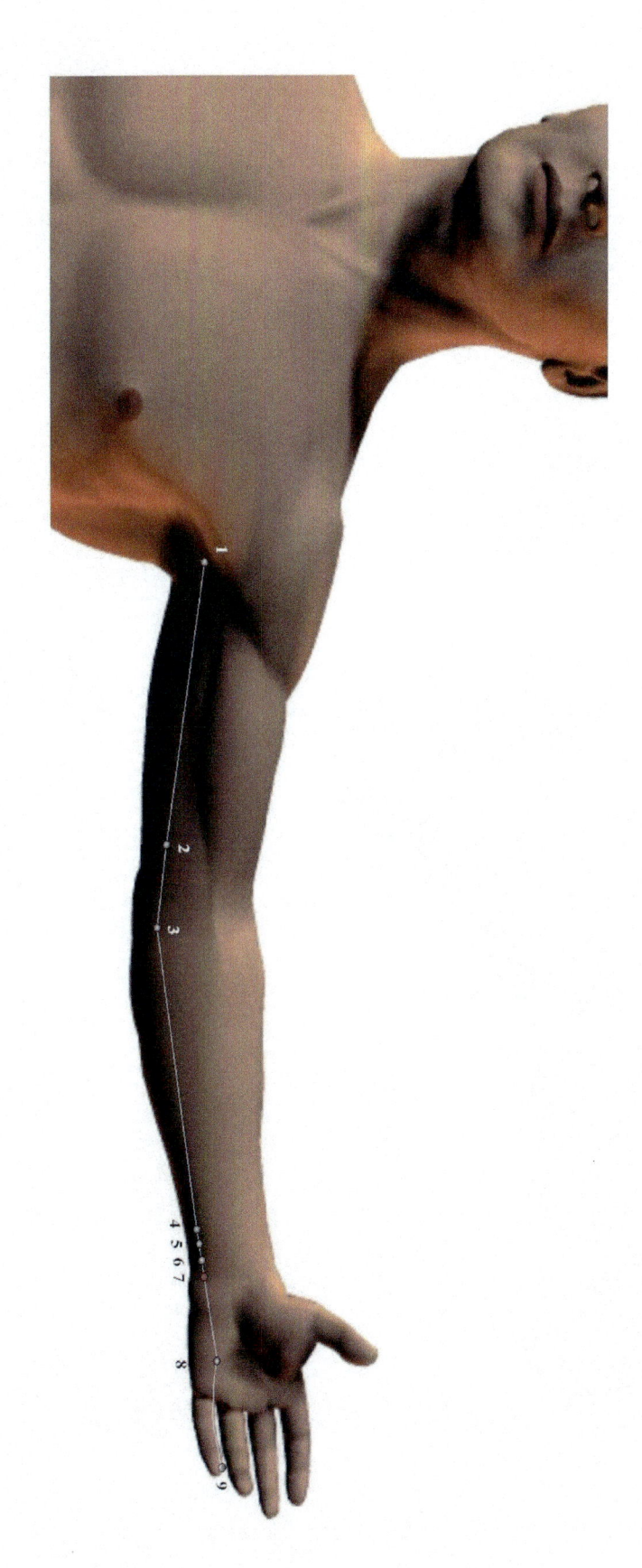

Bladder Meridian

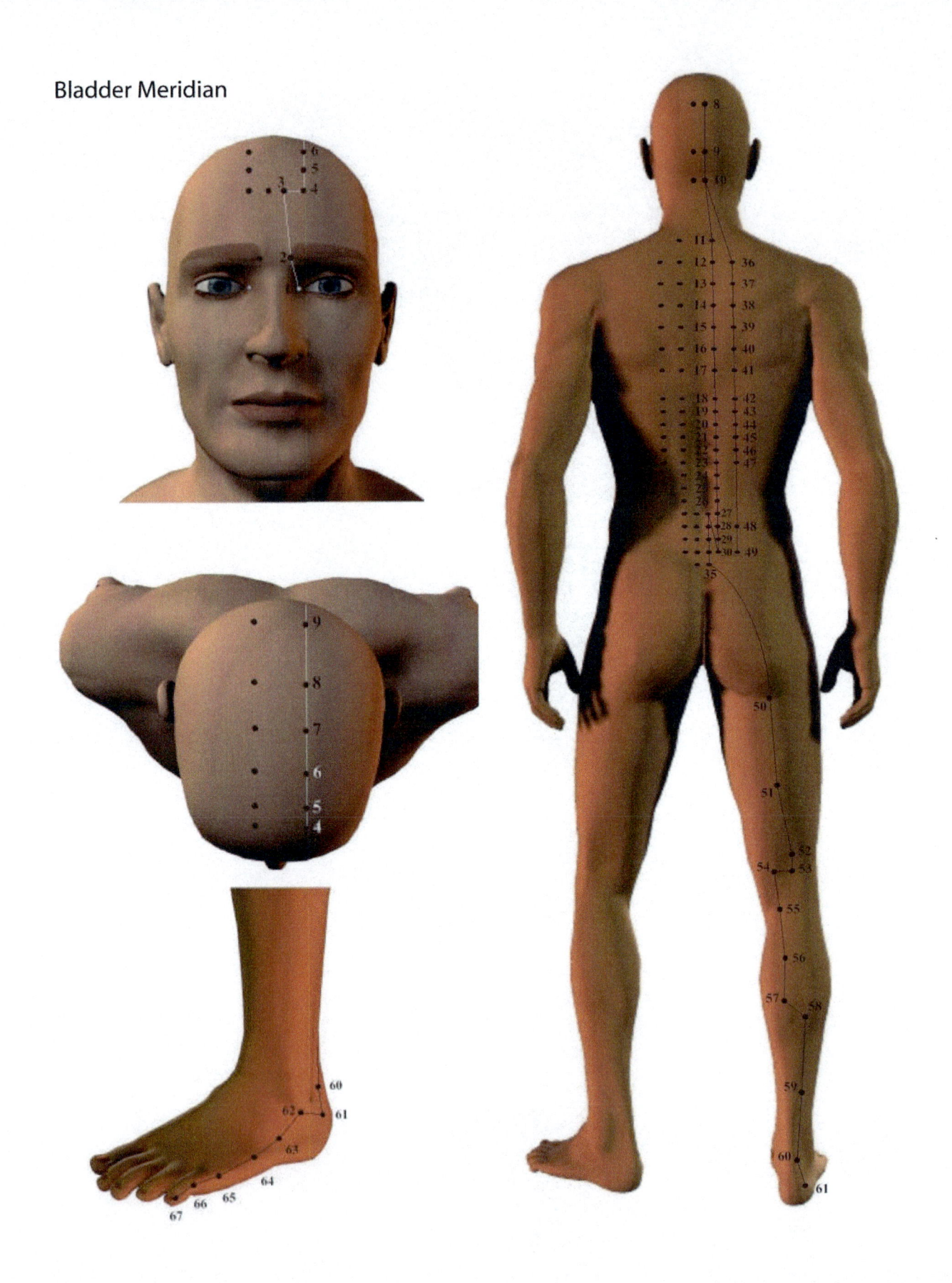

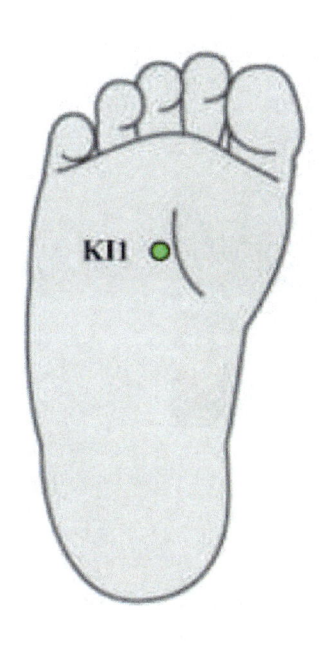

Kidney Meridian

81

Pericardium Meridian

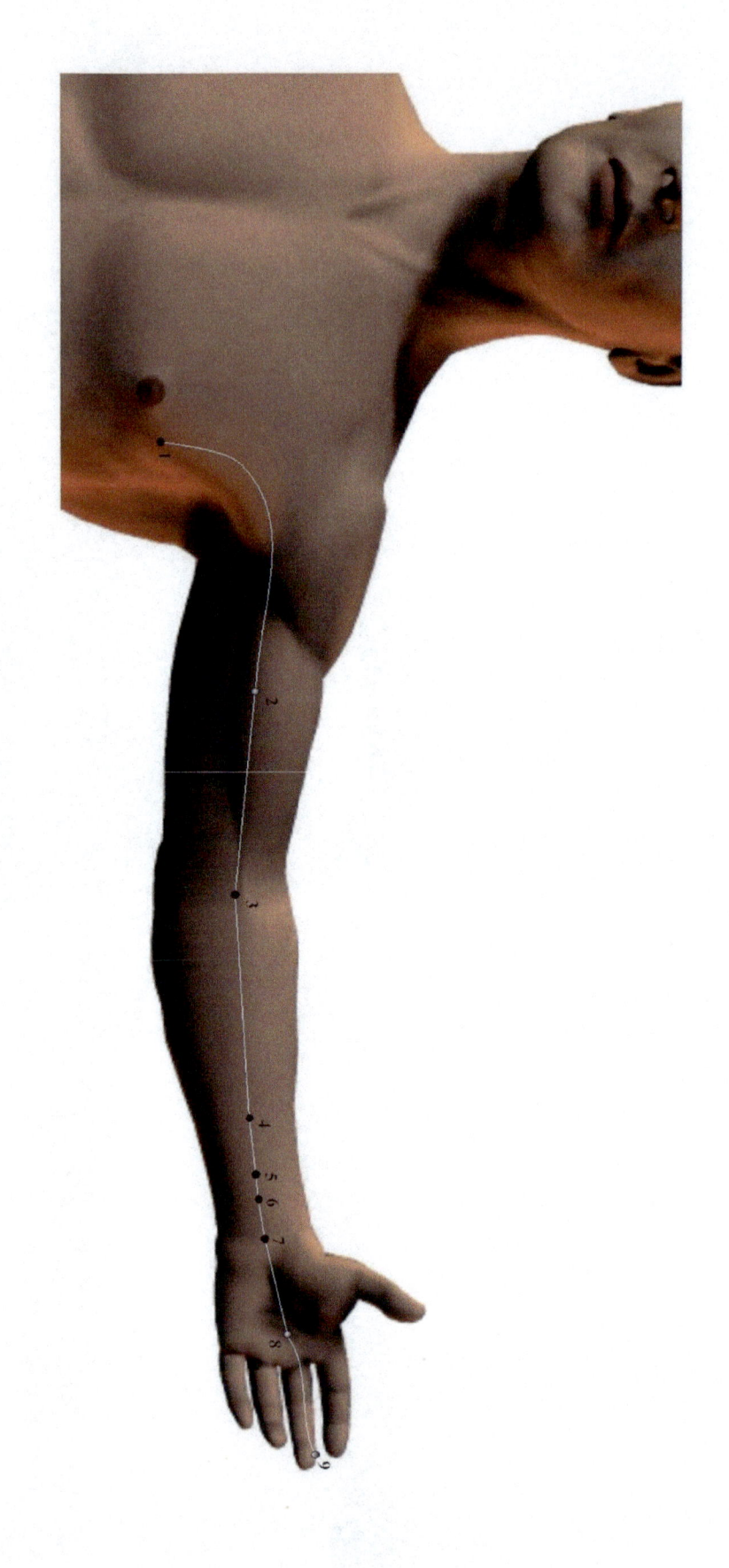

Triple Warmer Meridian

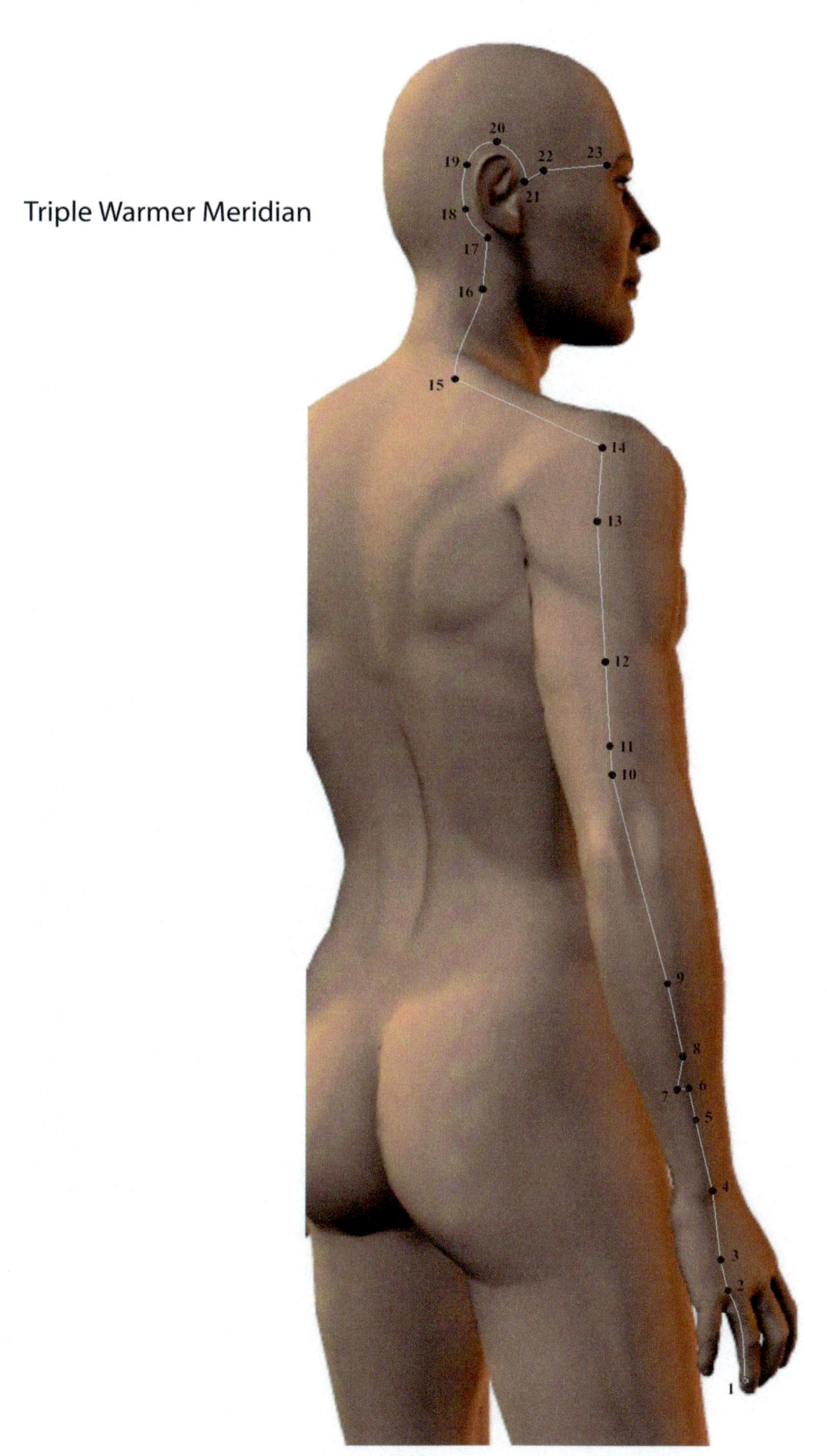

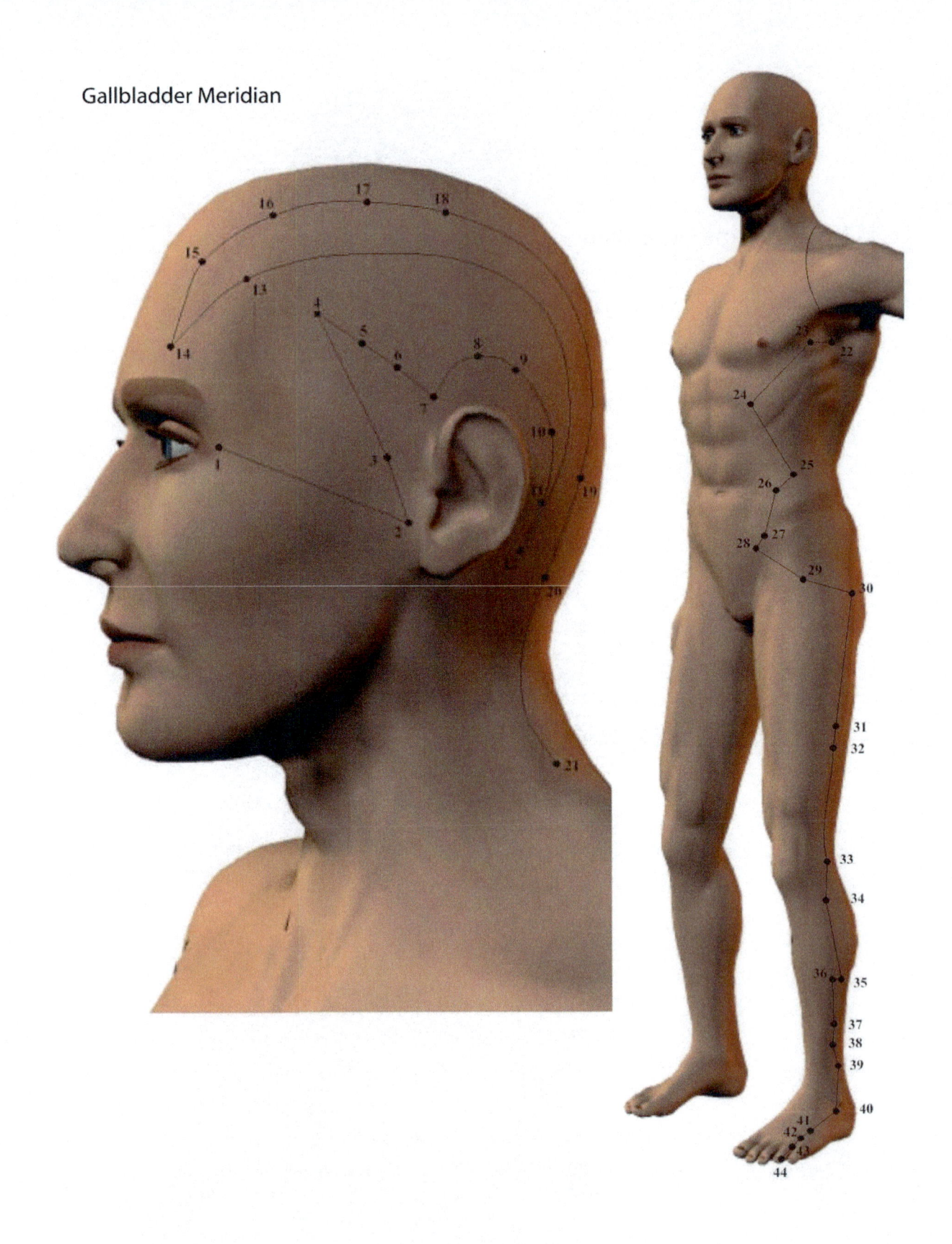

Gallbladder Meridian

Liver Meridian

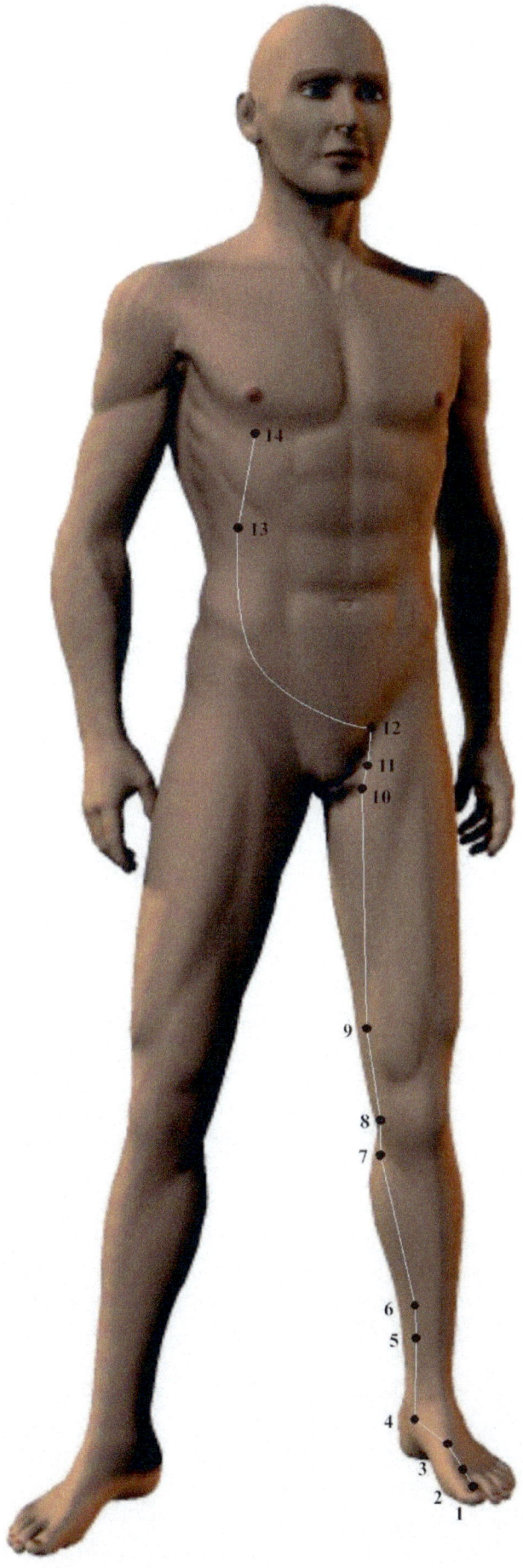

Notes

Kuden – Oral Teachings

A few examples of subjects covered in class for reference, in no particular order.

These articles are covered to highlight aspects of specific lessons, to serve as a reference point and to give context to certain martial, historical or terminology references you will encounter in your training.

It is not necessary to read through them all from first to last page as in a book, rather, just read the article which corresponds to the subject you are covering in that particular lesson.

Koi Carp & Perseverance

What is perseverance?
To endure, to continue with something even though it is difficult.
"If at first you don't succeed, try, try and try again".

The Japanese Kanji for endurance/perseverance is: Nin
It contains the characters for Strength and Heart or courage.
So, to persevere is to show you have a strong heart or have great courage in not giving up and trying to achieve your goals.

- Some things are easy to do, some are not.
- If we get angry and stop trying, we will never get better. We must persevere.
- Practicing things which require patience, helps us to learn to relax under pressure and to persevere with difficult tasks.
- Are there things you have had to persevere with, to improve?

In Japan, Koi Fish are often used to represent good fortune or luck. They are also associated with perseverance and strength of purpose and in Buddhism, the image of the Koi represents courage.

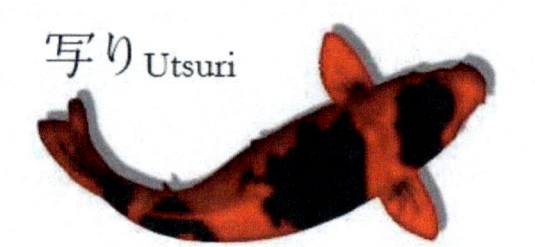

紅白
Kōhaku

写り Utsuri

According to legend, if a Koi fish succeeded in swimming up the waterfalls at a point called Dragon Gate on the Yellow River, it would be transformed into a water spirit – a Dragon. As Koi are said to regularly swim against the current and to swim up waterfalls, they have come to represent the pursuit of victory through hardship. Perseverance.

The Utsuri Obi (5th Dan) and Kohaku Obi (6th Dan) of Mizu Ryu Ju Jutsu take their names from the specific colour variations of Koi pictured above and the attributes of the Koi are reflected and personified by the holders of these special grades.

The learning of a Martial Art takes a long time. There are many repetitions to do in order to help you improve your technique. We may get it wrong many times, but what is important is we never stop trying to get it right. One day, we might get it right, but we will never stand a chance of getting it right if we do not persevere.

- **Write down 3 things you can do now, which you couldn't do at first.**
- **How did you feel when you finally achieved them?**
- **Write down 3 achievable things you would like to do but can't do just now.**
- **How do you think you will feel once you achieve them?**
- **Use the Problem-solving steps to identify and make a plan to achieve your goals.**

The Philosophy of Mizu Ryu Ju Jutsu

'Water is the fundamental essence of life. We should strive to attain the characteristics of water in our everyday life, as well as in our fighting spirit.

When sparing or fighting, we should have a fluency of movement and thought, similar to the motion of water. This gives us the ability to change our technique and thought processes with every change in attack from our opponent, therefore allowing us to make use of every opportunity as it arises.

Water adapts to its receptacle, as should we to every opponent, each attack and every problem we encounter in life.'

Anthony J Bailey, Shihan. Founder Mizu Ryu Ju Jutsu

Mizu Ryu Ju Jutsu Philosophy as written by
Master Calligrapher, Eri Takase, Shihan

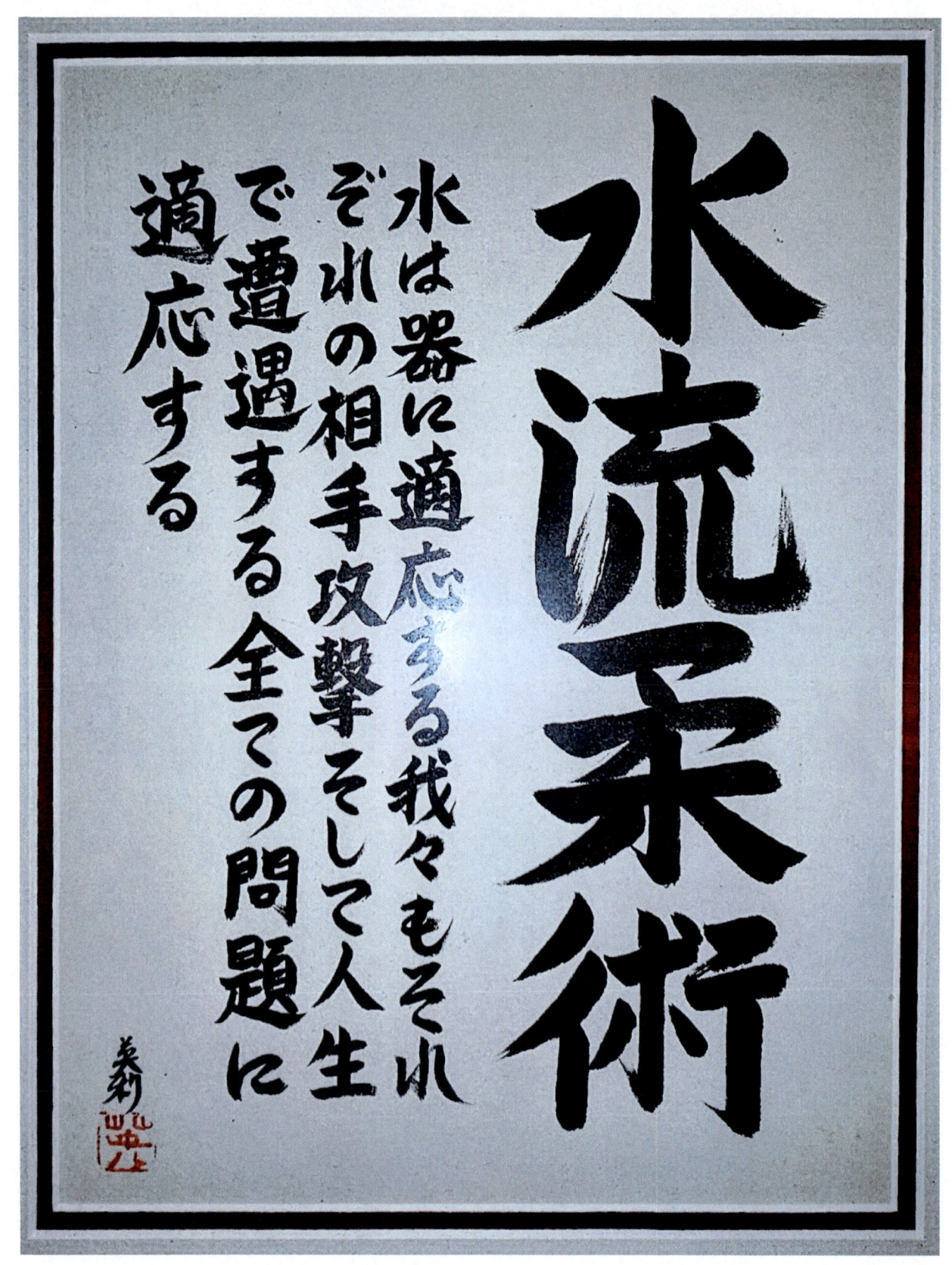

水流柔術

水は器に適応する我々もそれぞれの相手攻撃そして人生で遭遇する全ての問題に適応する

Mizu-ryu Ju Jutsu Principle philosophy
Shodo art piece translation by Eri Takase, Shihan

Below is the romanji reading for the Japanese.

水流柔術

mizu ryuu juu jutsu

水は器に適応する我々も

mizu wa utsuwa ni tekiou su ru ware ware

それぞれの相手攻撃 そして

so re zo re no ai te kougeki so shi te

人生で遭遇する全ての問題

jin sei de souguu su ru sube te no mon dai

に適応する

ni tekiou su ru

Mizu wa utsuwa ni tekiou suru wareware mo sore zore no aite kougeki soshite jinsei de souguu suru subete no mondai ni tekiou suru

This literally translates as;

Water adapts to its vessel, like we should with every attacking opponent, and every problem we encounter in life.

Biography - Eri Takase Shihan

Born and raised in Osaka Japan, Ms Takase trained in traditional Japanese calligraphy since the age of six devoting much of her life to the art. In 1989, Master Takase was awarded the rank of Shihan (or Master) in Japan's most prestigious calligraphic societies, the Bokuteki-kai and Bunka-shodo. In 1997 Master Takase founded her own school Takase Shodokai.

Master Takase is among the few to have won several best of category awards in national competitions and her work has been displayed in the Osaka Museum of Arts. To view this award winning art, please visit Traditional Japanese Calligraphy

In 1995, Master Takase moved to the United States and began transforming her art. Often quoted as saying, "Japanese Calligraphy is too beautiful a bird to be locked in the cage of a thousand years of tradition." She is also quick to add that the truly new comes from a respect and appreciation for what has come before. And so classically trained Ms. Takase's favorite expression is onkochishin or "Respect the past, create the new."

In 1998 Master Takase won positions in juried art shows including the prestigious 57th Street Art Fair in Chicago and Gasparilla Festival of the Arts in Tampa. But much more comfortable in the studio Ms. Takase gave up the life of the journey artist for the hectic serenity of the studio.

Along with her art she has been a columnist in several magazines including Martial Arts Insider Magazine and Kampsport.

This is not an advert, but for those with an interest, Takase Shihan has a website where you can purchase fine quality Japanese calligraphy. You can also contact her through the website to commission bespoke pieces, such as our club Instructors very kindly did for me with the Mizu Ryu calligraphy and translation to celebrate the club's 18th Birthday in 2012.

Takase Shihan's Website https://www.takase.com/

Buddhism & Martial Arts

This is not an in depth look at Buddhism. I only include some basic information here as so many aspects of Martial Arts make references to Buddhist characters and principles. I always encourage you to do your own research, question and discuss to form your own opinions. Use this information to find links in Martial teachings and explore them, or not, as you see fit.

Important Buddhist teachings
The 3 principal teachings are The 4 Noble Truths, The 8-Fold Path and Karma. As many of the links in Martial Arts are more Zen Buddhism than traditional Buddhism, some are more aligned to our studies than others. To go back to the milkshake analogy, Buddhism is milkshake, Zen is a flavour of that milkshake.

Zen vs Traditional
Traditional Buddhism forms the basis for Zen, but there are stark differences. For example, Zen doesn't teach reincarnation, karma or worship The Buddha. Zen teaches it is important to practice Zazen – seated meditation and extols the practice of mindfulness, to live in the present moment. Whilst traditional Buddhist monks are vegetarian, teetotal and celibate, many Zen Buddhists are not. A tool used in Zen for teaching, is Koans, a type of verbal riddle, statement or puzzle meant to create deep thought – *'What is the sound of one hand clapping?'* or our own Mizu Ryu Ju Jutsu Haiku. Enlightenment in Zen can come at any moment and doesn't rely on many years devoted to practice or reading scriptures. As such, Zen is concerned with a direct experience approach, not strict adherence to Buddhist writings.

Bodhidharma
Da Mo, Daruma or Bodhidharma, is perhaps the most famous Buddhist figure in Martial Arts. He was a priest from India, who brought Buddhist teachings to China in the 5th Century AD and founded Zen Buddhism.

Photo of a Bodhidharma scroll in my own home

The Zen outlook he brought to traditional Buddhism, together with the need for balance through rigorous physical training at the Shaolin Temple, means he is revered as the father of modern Martial Arts and his portrait hangs in many dojos to show that reverence.

Fudo Myo-o

A modern model of Fudo Myo-o I bought from a toy shop in Ueno, Japan

In Japan, the most renowned of the Godai Myo-o, the wrathful manifestations of the 5 Buddhas of Wisdom, is **Fudo Myo-o**. He is referred to as the 'immoveable' or 'unshakable' one, symbolically represented by the rock upon which he stands. He represents immutability, the steadfastness of his practice, conviction, belief and protection of, his faith.

His appearance and his weapons ward off demons and other inferior beings and frighten people back onto the path of righteousness. The flames behind him, are symbolic of the purpose of Buddhist concepts, mindfulness, meditation, The 4 Noble truths and The 8-fold path, as they represent purification of the mind in burning the material or emotional attachments that prevent humans reaching Enlightenment.

His sword is the sword of wisdom, to cut through ignorance, untruth and deceit to improve the chance of enlightenment. He also has a kind of lasso to catch and bind demons and those straying too far away from the Buddhist law.

He is regarded as a kind of Patron Saint of many Martial Arts schools. His eyes often left closed, right open and even his fangs (one facing up and one facing down) represent a pictorial reminder of Yin & Yang. He is often found at the centre of the other Godai Myo-o and is said to be venerated as a bringer of fortune for those who practice the 'money washing' ceremony at shrines. This is said to replicate and increase the money you wash, several times over, as long as you spend it within a week of the ceremony.

Kuji-ho

Kuji-ho is a set of mudras and mantras within the Mikkyo, esoteric arts of Shugendo, although it is said to originate from Taoism. Rare though it is in Martial Arts, in this form, parts of it are practiced within certain Ninjutsu, Kenjutsu and Ju Jutsu schools.

Kuji-in - Mudras

The fingers are entwined into intricate patterns to make the different mudras. Each has a name, and each has a mantra, or incantation. The diagram for Retsu here, is a mirror of the one most widely used, but there are many, many different variations of all mudras.

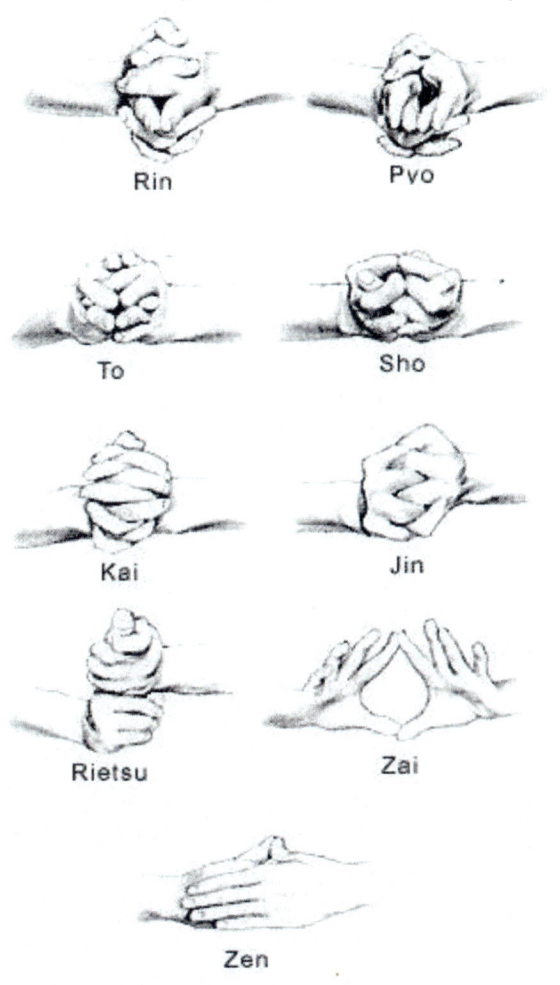

Rin   Pyo
To   Sho
Kai   Jin
Rietsu   Zai
Zen

English translations of the mantras

Rin – Strength of Mind and Body
Pyo – Direction of energy
To – Harmony with the Universe
Sho – Healing Self and others
Kai – Premonition of Danger
Jin – Knowing the thoughts of others
Retsu – Mastery of Time and Space
Zai – Controlling the elements of Nature
Zen – Enlightenment

Kuji-kiri

If making the incantation in the air or over a picture, for example, the 9-cuts are made with the symbolic sword hand, similar to Retsu, alternating between horizontal, then vertical for each of the 9 characters. A 10th character can be drawn within the grid and the entire image created a type of protection from something, or improving the focus of the individual, helping them achieve their goal, or to address an injury or illness in the mystical healing arts as taught at the Tenshin Shoden Katori Shinto Ryu.

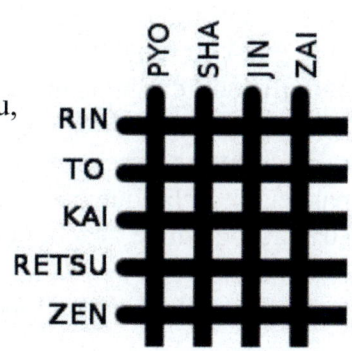

	PYO	SHA	JIN	ZAI
RIN				
TO				
KAI				
RETSU				
ZEN				

Shu Ha Ri

守破離

In Mizu Ryu Ju Jutsu, I am always reminding students that learning is on several levels and the emphasis and use of techniques changes, the more experienced you become. One aspect of this can be explained by the Japanese concept of Shu Ha Ri.

Of Shu Ha Ri, Aikido master Endō Seishirō Shihan stated:

'It is known that, when we learn or train in something, we pass through the stages of shu, ha, and ri. These stages are explained as follows:
- In shu, we repeat the forms and discipline ourselves so that our bodies absorb the forms that our forbearers created. We remain faithful to the forms with no deviation.
- Next, in the stage of ha, once we have disciplined ourselves to acquire the forms and movements, we make innovations. In this process the forms may be broken and discarded.
- Finally, in ri, we completely depart from the forms, open the door to creative technique, and arrive in a place where we act in accordance with what our heart/mind desires, unhindered while not overstepping laws.'

The shu ha ri concept was first presented by Fuhaku Kawakami as Jo-ha-kyū in Tao of Tea. Then, Zeami Motokiyo the master of Noh, extended this concept to his dance as Shu ha ri, which then became a part of the philosophy of Ju Jutsu, Aikido and Shorinji Kempo. Shu ha ri can be considered as concentric circles, with Shu within Ha, and both Shu and Ha within Ri. The fundamental techniques and knowledge do not change. The core stays the same as a solid foundation and the rest is built upon that solidity, as it is with our Mizu Ryu syllabus.

During the shu phase the student should loyally follow the instruction of a single teacher; the student is not yet ready to explore and compare different paths, but this is where many falter, thinking they are not learning quickly enough and look for a new teacher/style, not realising they are already getting what they need. Often, what we need is different to what we want.

So, realise that the training comes in many different levels, according to your own understanding and application at the time and that just learning how to do a technique is not enough. You must learn it faultlessly. Be able call upon it and use it at will, under different and difficult circumstances, as a single technique or as a counter, or as part of a combination whenever you decide. Then, let it leave your mind so you no longer consciously choose to do it. Your body can choose it without conscious thought when the circumstances best suit that particular technique out of the bank of 100's that you know, depending on the attack, speed, strength, balance, reach, height, weight etc of your opponent.

Learn the basics… Adapt and improve…Free yourself and flow.

Gokai Sansho

The 5 precepts here, were arranged by *Mikao Usui*, founder of the Japanese healing system called *Reiki* or *Te ate* as it was in his time. As a practice, it is similar to Martial Arts in that it is intent driven. Setting a good intention - *Mokunen*, at the start of the day is highly important and usually done during Mokuso. Set a good intention at the start of the day and keep trying to stick to it. Reaching the goal is good, continuing to try is very important.

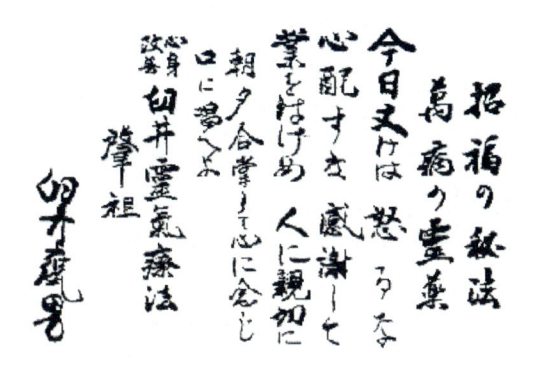

- Kyo Dake Wa — Just for today
- Okaru-Na — Don't get angry
- Shinpai-Suna — Do not worry
- Kansha-shite — Be humble
- Gyo o hage me — Be truthful in your dealings with others
- Hito ni shinsetsu ni — Be compassionate with yourself and others.

You say the *Gokai* – 5 Precepts, 3 times when you do *Mokuso* – Meditation.

If you want to learn how to say the precepts in Japanese, once you know how to pronounce them, make a note of how that might look in English. The following example is how someone used English phonetic sounds to try to remember how to pronounce the Japanese words, but make whatever notes make sense to you and which help you pronounce the words correctly.

Japanese   English

- Kyo Dake Wa — Kyoh dacky waa
- Okaru-Na — Ockaroo na
- Shinpai-Suna — Shin Pie soona
- Kansha-shite — Can sha shtay
- Gyo o hage me — Gyoh o hagay may
- Hito ni shinsetsu ni — He toe knee shin setsoo knee

Situational Awareness

'A conscious knowledge and understanding of all the elements in your immediate environment and the ability to forward project their likely outcomes. In other words, a dynamic risk assessment.'

We often discuss self-defence, the legal and moral aspects of when to and when not to use physical techniques and the necessary awareness needed to spot the onset of dangerous situations. This last aspect is perhaps one of the most important parts relating to self-defence. If you get this right, you won't be in the situation of being caught off-guard and may even make decisions which take you away from that dangerous environment before danger fully presents itself. This section cannot do justice to the whole teaching, but will serve as a reminder to the discussions had in class.

Mindset – Awareness levels

There are several ways of looking at this, but one of the easiest, yet most comprehensive is that of the Cooper Colour Code as formulated by the US Marine Jeff Cooper. He was a firearms instructor and taught extensively on Combat mindset and awareness levels. Here's a simple version to remind you of the different levels and what they represent.

Cooper Colour Code

White	Switched off, totally relaxed. Unaware of your surroundings
Yellow	Relaxed, yet aware of your surroundings. Prepared and able to notice changes
Orange	In alert mode having noticed a raised level or likelihood of threat. Verify and plan to evade or act
Red	Threat confirmed, actively engaged. Committed to active evasion or engaging the threat (Fight or Flight)
Black	Sensory overload. Unable to act or think (freeze)

White

Usually when people are in a safe place, at home, in comfortable and familiar surroundings, with no previous or currently present dangers. The sort of mindset which leads easily towards rest and sleep. Yet, there are occasions when people are negotiating public spaces in a very similar mindset and not aware of the dangers around them. How many people do you see walking in the street, completely glued to their phone screens, totally unaware of their surroundings!?

Yellow
The state of mind that a Martial Artist lives in for a large part of their lives. At least, they should do. Those who do not train or who have not trained for very long, misunderstand this as a mild state of paranoia, but that is not the case. Yellow state, is being aware of your surroundings – situational awareness. Scanning for hazards and determining risk as you go. It has many personal health and safety implications and is succinctly described in Japanese by the term ***Zanshin – A heightened state of relaxed alertness.***

Orange
The state in which you have identified a potential risk and you begin to plan a strategy to deal with this, whether by escape and evasion or by assessing a physical attack and defence. You are ready to interact, and actively involved in planning a route out of the situation or a planned physical intervention.

Red
The state where you are actively engaged in carrying out your plan – actually fighting or running away. You must have weighed up all options before committing to make sure you have the best chance of separating yourself from the danger and not running into an additional dangerous situation.

Black
Even with awareness and planning, some people are not able to cope well with the stress and anxiety associated with a dangerous situation. Like the proverbial rabbit in the headlights, they freeze due to sensory overload and can neither move nor think their way out of the situation. Training builds skill, strength, speed and confidence and sparing and realistic scenario training helps to condition better reflex responses, which in turn improve confidence, so, ***practice!***

Exercises for juniors (and adults!)
Whilst out and about, on a walk to the local shop or the park, on the way to school, even in a car journey, ask questions about the environment as you pass by.

- *How many people were at that bus stop?*
- *What colour hat was the man wearing as he was walking his dog?*
- *Are people blocking our entry or exit to a shop / cash machine and are there alternative routes?*

The list is endless, but it's a good observational game to play, which helps in paying attention to your surroundings, without raising it to high anxiety levels. Come up with your own observational questions, find different ways to practice the skill of being in a heightened state of relaxed alertness.
When in public, always be aware of your surroundings. Pay attention to panicked behaviour of crowds and make situational awareness your default mindset.

Tips for keeping children safe

Online, Phones, Tablets, PC, Games Consoles
With smart phones being in almost every school child's pocket and the internet more accessible than ever before, children can be at risk from harmful influences at school or at home, just as much as out in an unknown or dangerous location. With this in mind, as much as we might think these things are commonly understood, it is worthwhile taking time to have a conversation with your children, to ensure they are able to spot red flags and keep themselves safe in times where we are not even aware they are in danger.

So many children use the internet, chat groups, social media, even game consoles, to meet new people and gain new friends. Sometimes, the desire to find friendship, to speak with someone who 'gets them' or who says they have had the same experiences, or just speak with someone who improves their self-esteem with regular compliments, can blinker the view of otherwise switched on people. Most of the time, they will never meet these 'friends', but, unfortunately, there are an increasing number of cases whereby children have gone to meet an online friend for the first time, only to find out it's not who they thought it was. Profiles can be hacked or faked very easily. Just because a profile picture is of a 14-year-old girl called Casey, it doesn't mean it's them. It could just as easily be a 62-year-old called Jeffrey.

Research the sad cases of online grooming, leading to false imprisonment, controlling & coercive behaviour, bullying & blackmail:
Kayleigh Haywood https://youtu.be/WsbYHI-rZOE?si=_R1DIhm6CBNKpygH
Brek Bednar https://youtu.be/hZIYSCE-ZjY?si=1-E5hSpWVfJh8Vdt
Cyberbullying https://youtu.be/-Ho-MoPkIF4?si=7c52_WY5MWOQ_I7N
Webwise Ireland https://youtu.be/BjLgCuvWiJk?si=obKiMZIHYBAam26-

Talk to your children about being SMART

Safe – Never give out personal information when chatting or posting online. Personal information is things like: your name, your date of birth, your address, your phone number, your home address, your school name, your account details such as passwords or card or bank details. Also, be very careful when sending images as background information can also identify things about you and where you live. All this information in the wrong hands can make things difficult for you and can be used to create fake profiles to trap other victims.

Meet – Meeting someone you've only met online can be dangerous. If you really feel you need to meet this online friend, make sure you speak to your parents/guardian about it first and only go if they can come with you. Remember, online friends you've never met are still strangers, even if you've been chatting for a long time and really seem to 'click' together well.

Accepting – Accepting emails, messages, apps, opening files, images or texts from people you don't know can lead to problems. The content could be really terrible and nasty, or it could hold a virus which could either steal your personal information or damage or delete files from your phone, laptop, tablet or PC. If you have a home network, a sophisticated virus can attack everyone else's devices that use your Wi-Fi.

Reliable – Someone online can lie about who they are and what they know. Some information you find online might not be true. Pay attention to information that someone gives you about themselves, that changes over time. This is a good indication that the person is not genuine if they begin to forget parts of the story they have invented. Always check online information you are being pointed to, by using several sources, including books and other people, to get a wide variety of different information streams. Check information and research other reliable sources before forming your own opinion.

Tell – Tell a parent or guardian, teacher, club welfare officer or any other trusted adult, if something or someone online, makes you feel uncomfortable or worried. Also tell them if someone you've only met online is asking you to 'send photos', meet up with them or if you or someone else is being bullied online or being encouraged to self-harm too. Bullying in person is bad enough, but at least you can leave the location where it happens. It feels like there is no escape from online or cyber-bullying as you take your phone with you, everywhere. Telling a responsible adult can help to get any of these problems under control quickly and can also lead to prosecution if the person is found to be guilty of an offence.

Bullying
Most people recognise the 4 main types of bullying:
- **Physical bullying** - being assaulted, things thrown at them, spat at, possessions taken.
- **Verbal bullying** - name calling, teasing, threatening, inappropriate comments.
- **Social bullying** – leaving someone out on purpose, telling others to not speak to them, spreading lies and rumours, or deliberately embarrassing them in public.
- **Cyber bulling** - via text, chat groups, social media and other internet-based systems.

Sometimes, manipulative children will feign friendship in order to get something from the victim, i.e. information or photos, in order to use it against them. These days, a great deal of bullying goes on through cyber-bullying, it's easier to get away with for many at school than to risk getting into fights. The difference for the victim of cyber-bullying is, when they leave the physical bullying environment, they escape it, even if only temporarily till the next day. With cyber-bullying, they take it home with them as it's on their phone either directly, or they are seeing messages or photos posted about them, in chat groups or social media that others see and comment on.

Bullying is extremely harmful and can leave long-lasting effects into adulthood. It is generally perpetrated by those seeking to bolster their own self-esteem by robbing someone else of theirs, and it can drive some victims to depression, self-harm and even suicide.

Like prejudice, bullying can be a learned behaviour by way of **peer group pressure**, or to combat a **trauma** they have experienced, or it can be something that is learned from **family attitudes and beliefs**. Regardless of the reason or the type of bullying, it should be treated the same way. It is unacceptable and needs reporting and dealing with as soon as possible.

If you or anyone else you know is experiencing bullying of any nature, report it!

Report it to a teacher, a parent, your club instructor, a responsible adult or even online at any one of the help lines or websites listed in this chapter.

Grooming

Most of you will have heard about online grooming from several media sources. You may be unaware though, just how much this happens and the lengths to which groomers go to select and 'train' their victims. In addition, not all groomers fit the stereotype of dirty, older men, sat in a basement.... there's actually a great deal more grooming going on from narcissistic children / teenagers of both sexes (and all genders!) than most people would think. This helps mask the issue as most adults would not suspect a young teenager of wanting to, or being able to, act in this way. There are signs you should look out for, which may help you identify potential problems, but it can be very difficult to tell. Grooming is a coercive and controlling behaviour. It survives on keeping the victim from asking for help, as they invariably don't understand they need help, until it's too late.

The *Internet Matters Organisation* lists the following things to be aware of but, be aware that some of these are 'normal' behaviour for growing children/teenagers.

- Spending more and more time on the internet
- Being secretive about the sites they visit and who they are talking to online.
- Switching screens, logging off or shutting down when you come near.
- Phones/tablets etc they have which you didn't give them.
- Using sexual language that unusual for them and is out of character.
- Becoming emotionally volatile.

Take control

- Have ongoing conversations with your children about staying safe online.
- Use a 'family account' and parental controls to restrict access to certain internet sites.
- Make use of safety tools on internet browsers and social media networks.
- If they have social media profiles, make sure they haven't falsified their D.O.B.
- Turn on safety or child modes for search engines and sites such as YouTube.
- Make sure they know to get immediate screenshots of anything that needs reporting.
- Speak to school or college welfare officers if you have concerns as they can also monitor behaviour and initiate other conversations around safety.
- Use a parental tracking app for your child's phone, and make sure their devices and profiles are not set to publicly share real-time location.

Narcissistic & emotional control

Sometimes, unhealthy relationships are started and controlled by those who have already chosen their victim and as such, the victim may be completely unaware that they are being groomed or controlled. It's also been known that narcissists quite often choose 'strong' victims as a way to boost their own ego by 'conquering' them, proving they are stronger.

Emotional control is key here, as it is through this that the perpetrator builds trust with the victim, as well as sowing the seeds to isolate them from family and friends who might discover and stop what is going on. With narcissistic or emotional control, it's not always about being externally bullied. Sometimes it's more subtle than that and relies on mental and emotional manipulation. Sometimes the perpetrator will play the victim, to gain support, sympathy and trust and use passive-aggressive behaviour to control their victim. *(Check States of Mind, session 1, p107 of Tools for Problem Solving).*

Real-life example of coercive control
In some cases, one in particular I've dealt with for a former student, emotional blackmail was used as a weapon to gain control. After having gained trust and emotional dependency, the perpetrator used the threat of violence against family members to maintain control. Whilst the victim was more than able to physically defend themselves, the perpetrator stalked their home and family movements, following the mother to work and younger sibling to school, to underline the fact that they couldn't be there for everyone. This is the way some will gain compliance. It's not as easy as saying, just punch them as the perpetrator has made it clear any attempt to stand up to them or end the relationship, will end in retaliation against family members who are unable to defend themselves. This resulted in several violent incidents as the victim had been convinced that if they defended themselves, others would get hurt.

In this case, the victim finally told me what was going on, I worked with the victim and their family, involved Police and counselling and my team and I acted to ensure they were kept safe. It was all successfully resolved in a court case.

Help and Resources
There are lots of online resources and telephone advice lines available to you and your children. The more you research, the more you will be able to identify when help is needed. Search online for more information, signs to look out for, strategies, help and advice.

CEOP	Child Exploitation and Online Protection A specific branch of Police who deal with online abuse and exploitation of children, up to the age of 18 years old. Website: www.ceop.police.uk/safety-centre/
NSPCC	Leading UK children's charity, they give help and advice on Bullying, abuse, self-harm and anything which has put a child in danger. Lots of information on their website and you can contact advisors for support and information. Tel: 0808 800 5000 Website: www.nspcc.org.uk
Childline	NSPCC's telephone support service. They have online counsellors to talk through issues and a separate section online for children under 12 years old. Tel: 0800 11 11 Website: www.childline.org.uk
Shout 85258	A text Crisis line for anyone to text about any kind of worries they have which are putting them into crisis. Often used by people who are stressed, anxious, suffering bullying or abuse as well as those who self-harm, feel depressed or who have suicidal thoughts. Trained volunteers can help deescalate your emotional response to situations and help you discover healthier ways to deal with the issues you face. Text SHOUT to 85258 to start an online chat

Always, if in immediate danger, call 999

There are many other organisations that deliver similar services. These subjects can be difficult to face or deal with but, as we know from our Martial Arts training, we don't run away from difficulty, we keep trying to overcome it.

Raising alarm discretely
The Canadian Women's Foundation (CWF) created a discreet hand signal for victims of domestic abuse, who's only contact with the outside world was webcam during the Covid-19 pandemic. It was decided that a hand signal, if universally recognised, would give the victim the chance to indicate they needed help, without the need for verbalising it or tipping off their captor. This quickly gained worldwide recognition through TikTok and today it is used by anyone, regardless of age, who finds themselves in a difficult, captive or abusive situation and is unable to speak about it whilst under the control of their captor.

Distress Hand Signal
1. Hold the fingers of one hand open
2. Fold the thumb to the palm of the hand
3. Cover the thumb with all the fingers.

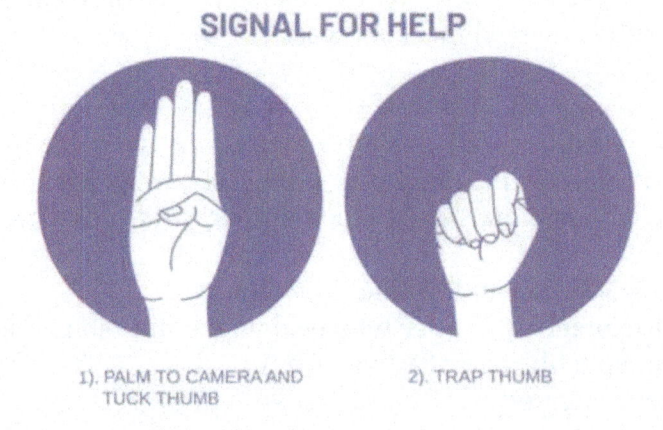

SIGNAL FOR HELP

1). PALM TO CAMERA AND TUCK THUMB

2). TRAP THUMB

Repeat this 3-step process to send the signal

CWF Video - https://youtu.be/AFLZEQFIm7k?si=XCcZM0MNfgu0fZUX

The person in distress, could be making this sign behind their back, whilst shopping with their 'parent'. We are conditioned to accept that a child walking around a shop with an adult, is normally with their parent, but this is not always the case.

Check out this staged example, to give you context. Yes it is staged, but it shows the physically controlling behaviour and how, if people recognise and learn this signal, it is more likely someone can intervene, either themselves or by calling the Police.

https://youtube.com/shorts/ZUoVbLazKVA?si=cLEFkdzolNWfvgxS

This is a real case of abduction where the victim was saved by making this sign in a shop and the staff member recognised the sign and alerted the Police.
https://youtu.be/i3VnF5cT2S4?si=4mPToEvLvnrc2SH

Remember it and teach it to your children.

If you ever see it being used, but don't feel capable of intervening yourself, take photos / selfies including the people involved, any vehicles or registration number plates and contact the Police immediately.

Self-harm
This is a difficult subject for some to face or even to try to understand. I am not intending to scare you with this, but as we know, we face issues, not run away from them. Without the knowledge of what we're facing, how can we ever work to minimise or alleviate it? Self-harm amongst young children and teenagers is massively increasing, or at least, the number of cases reported is increasing. Yes, I know those are 2 different things and it's good that it is being talked about, but it's not good that some are seeing Self-harm as a 'normal' way to deal with difficult situations.

What is self-harm and why do they do it?
It's usually the first question someone asks when they find out. WHY? There are several reasons why someone uses Deliberate Self Harm (DSH) to cope:

- Depression
- Anxiety
- Eating disorders
- Low self-esteem
- Bullying
- Abuse (mental, emotion, physical, sexual, substance)
- Grief
- Relationships
- Lack of direction and many others.

In fact, it can be different for each person and for some, they might not even know why they do it, other than when they do, it seems to release some form of tension that they experience.

Whilst most children will hide it very well, they may well be having conversations with others who do it and even share techniques. In addition, much like unsuitable websites, chat groups, apps, films & TV series, there are some which actively promote self-harm and suicide. Imagine, if the person giving advice either in txt, chat or via an app, is a narcissistic sociopath who is deliberately leading vulnerable people to self-harm. It happens. We heard of this on a worldwide scale 4 or 5 years ago, when a news story from Russia broke about the Blue Whale Challenge. It isn't fiction, it happens, and this leads us back to online safety.

How do they self-harm?
Figures show that 80% of people who report self-harming, do so with some sort of sharp object. It can start as scratching, but usually involves cutting the skin, surface level, in a place you don't often see, or is easy to cover up, such as the arms or legs. Tell-tale signs of blood spots on tissues or bedclothes may be an indication, but conversations are needed to find more information. Other common forms are overdoses, punching hard objects, picking at skin, pulling own hair, swallowing foreign bodies and burning parts of the body.

There are many everyday objects in the household which can hold an edge and even if no one in the house smokes, other everyday items can cause burning. If we did find something which is being used to create self-harm and merely confiscated it, the chances are, that person will just find something else potentially more damaging to use if we don't address the cause. So, as we know we can't rid our world of potentially damaging objects, we are better off changing the coping strategy and therefore guiding them towards making healthier choices.

We need to help them find healthier ways to deal with those stressful thoughts, feelings and emotions. Rather than try to 'scare them out of it' or coming across as aggressive, try to understand what's going on by looking at it from their view. We need to stay calm and open so we can **Communicate**. We don't need to agree with their opinion, to **Empathise**. We need to offer support and be strong enough to **Ask for help**.

Communication, Empathy and Asking for help
Make sure they know you are open to talking about it, but also, give them space. You'll be far more successful ensuring they know you are able to talk in a calm, supportive frame of mind than going off on one, pressuring them to talk when they are not ready, and making them withdraw. As I said before, they may not even know or be able to express why they do what they do, so, you may need to give them time to find the words before a conversation can take place. Eventually, you can build towards creating an agreed list of actions like: *they agree to tell you if they have self-harmed,* or *when they feel like doing it they come and talk to you,* or *if they don't feel comfortable talking to you they can talk to someone else about it.* Through open **communication**, build a ladder together, towards healthier coping methods.

You don't need to have committed the same acts yourself to understand the contributing factors. We all know what stress, anxiety, frustration, rage, loneliness and sadness feels like. Concentrate on that to help you to **empathise** and you'll understand that the person who is self-harming, is feeling ordinary human emotions that you or I can feel, it's just that they are using unhealthy ways of coping with it.

Don't forget, there are loads of professional resources available to help, with advice and support for both parents and children alike. Your GP can be a point of call if you are worried as can any number of the support services I've mentioned. **YPI Counselling in Basingstoke** are a brilliant counselling service for children, but there is a 6-month waiting list after application! What's important, is to not take it all on by yourself and to **ask for help**. Start by finding out more from national guidelines and websites like the one's in this chapter and go from there. Asking for help is not only helping to look after the child, but also to look after yourself too. You can't help if your own mental health declines to the point at which you are unable to help, so don't forget to seek support for yourself too.

Summary of keeping children safe
Self-Defence isn't just about punches and kicks. Sometimes, self-defence *is* about defending yourself from someone else. But, sometimes, self-defence is defence *<u>from</u>* the self. As unpleasant as it might be to think about the subjects in this chapter, it is important to think about them and know what to look out for. Communication is key, but it has to be two-way. It also needs to be non-confrontational and non-judgemental, or you risk making things worse. We have only covered the surface of a wide and deep issue, but hopefully this chapter gives you a start to help you identify problems, make a plan and know who to ask for help.

Work through the Problem-Solving Tools, week by week, in the next chapter. Take time to follow the exercises and use the tools it teaches, to solve the problems in this chapter, or any other problems you come across. Our Welfare officer can be the first port of call for anyone in the club who is experiencing difficulty with issues raised in this chapter, or you can use any of the resources already mentioned. Whatever the issue, **Communicate & Ask for help.**

Tools For Problem Solving

Session 1 - State of mind - mental & emotional attitudes

Introduction
The information and exercises in this chapter, build problem-solving skills, bit by bit, over several weeks. Don't try to go through the whole lot in one go as you need time to think about each session you work through and embed the learning. Don't just read through the pages, follow and work on the exercises with examples which are personally relevant to you. Set time aside and give serious thought and effort – a good intent, to working on these exercises. In Martial Arts, we often talk about having a strong intent, determination and perseverance. These things determine how we go about trying to achieve our goals. Our success in achieving those goals, or solving problems or barriers which block us from achieving those goals, can be massively influenced by our state of mind. When we talk about someone's state of mind, or their mental attitude, what do think we mean?

As individuals, with different experiences, we deal with situations in different ways, but there are some common things we are all influenced by when we make decisions about things. When faced with difficulty, or problems, 2 main things dictate how we solve those issues:

The experiences from our past – what we've grown up seeing, hearing, learning & doing
The experiences from our present – what we're thinking, feeling, doing & experiencing now

These things help to make up our state of mind, our mental and emotional attitude towards solving problems or setting goals. We tend to settle into a set way of dealing with problems or setting goals that we've used in the past. But what is the danger with always doing things the way we've always done them in the past?

If things have worked for us in the past, that's good, but we should still check each time, to see if there is a better way of dealing with that situation, so we can improve.

If things haven't worked out for us and we've never worked out why, just hidden our head in the ground like an Ostrich, what happens to that problem we're hiding from?
With its head underground, the Ostrich can't see the issue, but when the Ostrich pops it's head up again, the problem is still there. It didn't go away and it still has to be dealt with.
A Martial Artist is involved in the constant pursuit of perfection, even though we know we are not likely to reach it. But it doesn't stop us from trying. We can't hope to achieve this without constantly checking for improvements. What is key here, is that we keep trying, putting into effect that 'persistent determination' I always talk about.

Being aware of our attitude or state of mind, will help us to understand why we're not getting the results we want when trying to solve problems or set goals and to change our efforts when we recognise we are in the wrong state of mind. We can easily point to other things or other people as being the problem, but sometimes, it's our own attitude or state of mind which is stopping us from making progress or finding a good solution to a problem. This is where the microcosm of Martial Arts and personal development, mirrors the macrocosm of life and interpersonal relationships.

In order to understand ourselves, other people and how we interact with each other, we'll look at some of the more common attitudes we come across. We need to look at what these different attitudes mean, how we see them and how as a state of mind, they affect our judgement, our decision making and the affect they have on the people around us:

Common attitudes or states of mind
Passive
Aggressive
Passive-aggressive
Assertive

Passive State of Mind

A passive state of mind can also be referred to as avoidant.
What does it mean to avoid something or someone?
Someone who is in the passive state of mind is fearful.

- Being fearful of making a decision or dealing with a situation because of <u>*unknown consequences*</u>.
- Being fearful of setting a goal because they <u>*fear not achieving it*</u>.
- Being fearful of talking to other people or talking about how you feel because of what others *might* think about you.
- The passive person is so fearful of upsetting others that they will often make decisions which are bad for themselves, just <u>*so they don't upset other people*</u>.

How do you think being in a passive state of mind impacts our decisions?
Are there positives or negatives to being in a passive state of mind?
Which famous person, cartoon or film character would you say represents a passive state of mind? Write their name, add or draw a picture of them.

Aggressive state of mind

Someone can be aggressive because they don't know many other ways to deal with problems. It can also be because that person feels the need to control what others do or say, or are fearful and use aggression to hide that fear from others.
What things do we notice about someone who is aggressive?

- Being *quick to anger*, most of the time seeming to be *for no good reason*.
- Being fearful of making a decision or dealing with a situation because of *unknown consequences* so they use anger / aggression *to intimidate others* into accepting their decision, even if it is wrong.
- Being fearful of talking to other people or talking about how you feel because of how others *might* think about you – using aggression to *keep people at a distance* and stop them from seeing your true thoughts and feelings.
- The Aggressive person *doesn't care* about the way their decisions affect other people, as long as *they get what they want* and *stop others from disagreeing*.
- Another common factor is the desire to control – using aggression to control other people's thoughts and their choices.

How do you think an aggressive state of mind impacts our decisions?
Are there positives or negatives to being in an aggressive state of mind?
Which famous person, cartoon or film character would you say represents an aggressive state of mind? Write their name, add or draw a picture of them.

Passive-aggressive state of mind

People who are passive-aggressive use emotional triggers to assert that control we see in the aggressive state of mind, but by seemingly non-aggressive means.
What things can we notice about someone who is being passive-aggressive?

- When someone wants you to agree to something you don't want to do and *they make you feel guilty* for not agreeing with them.
- *Throwing a tantrum or sulking* when you don't agree to something they want.
- *Ignoring you* or *getting others to ignore you* when you don't agree with them.
- Purposely saying or doing things to anger or upset you, then *playing the victim* when you react.

The action is passive, not overtly aggressive, but the intent behind the action is *to control the thoughts and choices of other people*. Their actions are designed to *make you feel unwanted or guilty* enough, to change your mind and agree to their demands. It is a form of control or manipulation and as such, it is now listed by The American Psychiatric Association in DSM-IV, as a Personality Disorder.

How do you think passive-aggressiveness impacts our decisions?
Are there positives or negatives to being in a passive-aggressive state of mind?
Which famous person, cartoon or film character would you say represents a passive-aggressive state of mind? Write their name, add or draw a picture of them.

Assertive state of mind

What does it mean to be in an assertive state of mind?
Someone who is assertive is usually confident and clear about what they need or want but there are differences between assertive and aggressive states of mind.
What things can we notice about someone who is being assertive?

- They can put their point across in a _confident, fair and balanced_ way because they have thought about what they want and how that impacts other people.
- They think it is still _important to listen to others_ and consider what others have to say, even if they have different needs.
- They are _prepared to discuss_ and negotiate with others just in case there is another opinion that is better, but will put their point across _without resorting to anger or manipulation_.
- An assertive person is _not afraid to 'stand up'_, to put their point across or to make suggestions. _Their confidence inspires confidence in others_ and they try to help people and solve problems rather than ignore them.

How do you think being assertive impacts our decisions?
Are there positives or negatives to being in an assertive state of mind?
Which famous person, cartoon or film character would you say represents an assertive state of mind? Write their name, add or draw a picture of them.

Exercise – Understanding states of mind

Scenario: You are in a supermarket and suddenly you feel yourself being pushed over by someone behind you. You stand up and see the person who pushed you…

1.1 How would someone in a passive state of mind react?
What might they feel in their body?
What thoughts might they say to themselves?
What might they say to the other person?
What might the passive person do?

1.2 How would someone in an aggressive state of mind react?
What might they feel in their body?
What thoughts might they say to themselves?
What might they say to the other person?
What might the aggressive person do?

1.3 How would someone in a passive-aggressive state of mind react?
What might they feel in their body?
What thoughts might they say to themselves?
What might they say to the other person?
What might the passive-aggressive person do?

1.4 How would someone in an assertive state of mind react?
What might they feel I their body?
What thoughts might they say to themselves?
What might they say to the other person?
What might the assertive person do?

States of mind summary

Having looked at a few of the more common things which give us clues as to our state of mind, it's important to concentrate on how our state of mind impacts our ability to solve problems, to set goals for ourselves and how we interact with other people. Being passive or aggressive, is not the best state of mind to be in, when trying to solve problems. Being assertive gives us a better chance of being clear about our needs, achieving our goals, considering options and measuring the impact of our decision for us and those around us.

An athlete may use aggression as a tool, in order to compete or succeed in a given physical task, but that is not the same as being an aggressive person. As with many things we study in Martial Arts, this awareness is useful not only within our combat or competitive arena, but also just as useful in social interaction and communication outside the dojo, in everyday life. Being aware of our thoughts, feelings, emotions and actions brings our attention to the problem because of the way we are reacting to it. This gives us the chance to use different tools to make measured decisions which are thoughtful, less impulsive and likely to have more successful outcomes.

Session 2 – The 6 Problem solving steps

Step 1 Recognising a Problem

In order to solve a problem, we have to first understand or recognise that there is a problem to solve. That sounds very obvious, but sometimes, we don't actually realise there is a problem until it's too late. Looking back at a situation can often reveal to us that there was a problem, way before we actually noticed it. Being more aware of what is going on in our lives, mental, emotional and physical cues as well as the way other people interact with us, can give us an early indication that there is a problem.

To do this, we must ask ourselves 4 questions:

What are my thoughts?
What am I feeling?
How am I behaving?
How are others behaving towards me?

What state of mind could you be in, if you are thinking…?
'Just shut up!'
'I'm going to smack you in the mouth in a minute!'
'I'll just do whatever they want, it's easier that way'
'I hope they're not going to ask me'
'You'll change your mind when I don't speak to you for 3 days'

What state of mind could you be in, if you are feeling…?
Pulse / heartbeat is racing
Butterflies in the stomach
Frustrated
Calm
Guilty
Jealous / resentful
Angry

What state of mind could you be in, if you are doing…?
Pacing
Clenched fists
Hot / flushed
Slouching
Constantly apologising and speaking softly
Standing straight with good eye contact

What state of mind could you be in, if others are…?
Keeping conversations short
Finding other things to do at short notice
Agreeing to everything and anything you say
Physically flinching when you move suddenly
Not giving direct eye contact
Constantly apologising to you
Losing patience and insulting you

You will notice that some of these can potentially indicate more than one state of mind, attitude or emotion. That's why we have 4 questions. Combining answers from all these questions, gives us a better indication of what's going on, as one single answer can be ambiguous.

Step 1 summary
Being aware of our cues, asking ourselves those questions: What are my thoughts? What am I feeling? How am I behaving? and How are others behaving towards me? gives us the information we need to recognise if there is a problem that we are reacting to and if we are in the right state of mind to solve that problem. Once we realise there is a problem and we recognise which state of mind we are in, we can see how this problem affects the things which are important to us and use other tools to help change that state of mind if necessary. This gives us a better chance of setting and reaching our personal goals, solving problems and using healthier communication with other people.

Session 3 – The 6 Problem solving steps

Step 2 Define the present, set the future

To help solve problems or achieve goals, it is important to start by objectively describing or taking notice or where we are now and what our future will look like once we solve the problem or reach our goal. There is a divide between these 2 aspects, that divide is the solution, the means by which we solve our issue or achieve our goal. Let's first start by making sure we have a clearly defined beginning and end to our problem. The solution will be easier to define, once we know exactly what is going on that requires change and what we want to achieve.

For this exercise, we'll use the analogy of crossing a large pond. In Kyoto, there is a beautiful, large shrine complex called Heian shrine. It has bright red buildings, bright white gravel on the ground and large ponds in the garden.
To get from one part of the pond to the other, there are stepping stones across the water.

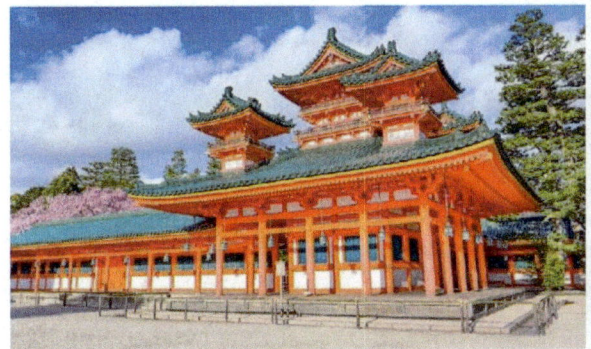

Our side of the pond is where we start from, where we are now.
Using the information from Step 1 (the questions we ask ourselves), let's put that information on our side of the pond.
Noticing what is going on now is a way of being Mindful, clearly defining the present.

On the other side of the pond, we can see where we want to be. Our goal.
On that side, let's put all the things we know about what we will be thinking, feeling, doing and how life will look once we have achieved our goal.

Two banks of the pond

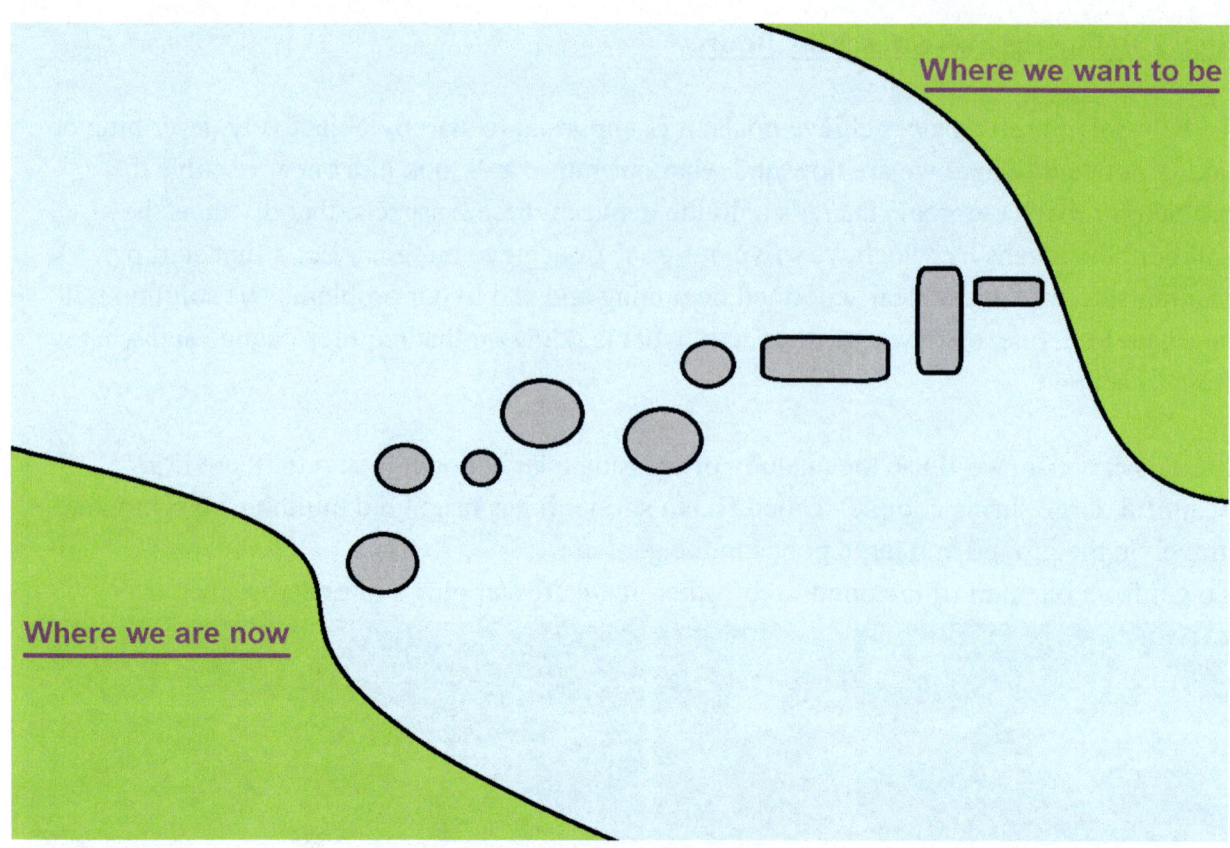

You can add your answers to the questions onto each bank of the pond, or you can write up a column list, or draw pictures for where we are now and where we want to be. For now, just clearly define these two banks of the pond. We will define the stepping stones between the banks in the next couple of exercises.

Where I am now		Where I want to be
What am I thinking? What am I feeling? How am I behaving? How are others behaving towards me? Is there a problem?		What will I be thinking? What will I be feeling? What will I be doing? How will others be behaving with me? What does life look like after solving my problem?

Step 2 summary

As stated in the beginning, to help solve problems or achieve goals, it is important to start by noticing where we are now and what our future will look like once we solve the problem or reach our goal.

Now that we have looked at questioning ourselves in order to harvest this information, fill in those answers for yourself by either making your own diagram or list of the two banks of the pond. Leave the centre column or a space for the steps and we will fill them out later.

Working through this exercise, we are already starting to utilise different problem-solving skills. Two of the most important tools being used are:

Mindfulness – being present in the moment, recognising what we are feeling, doing and where we are now
Goal setting – clearly defining what we want, where we want to be, how that feels and what life will be like when we achieve that goal.

Once we are more fully aware of our present situation and have clearly defined what our future goal looks and feels like, we can work on the steps between them – what we do, to reach our goals.

Session 4 – The 6 Problem solving steps

Step 3 Getting evidence

The next part in our problem-solving steps, is looking at the information we have and separating fact from fiction. To have a good chance of being successful in solving a problem or achieving our goal, we must base our decisions on factual evidence, not assumptions or hearsay. Sometimes, following what other people say about a particular thing or situation, without questioning, researching or testing evidence, can cause us more problems than we started with. So, the next step in our process is to check and decide what information we have is *assumption* and what is backed by *evidence*. In this day and age of memes and viral social media opinions, this part is massively underutilised.

As mentioned before, we are all influenced by things from our past as well as the present and these biases can skew the way we see situations and the help or advice we give to others. Even if well meaning, some of the advice we gain from others might not help as much as intended. On the other hand, some advice is invaluable and comes from a place of great experience. How then, do we tell the difference?

There are 4 things we need to consider here, all of which, can feed into each other:

- **What I know for sure**
- **What I've heard from others**
- **What I think I know**
- **What I need to find out**

Let's look at how these things help us to separate out assumption and to highlight information which is evidence based, to help solve our problem.

Snakes & Ladders of evidence

What I <u>know</u> for sure
This box of information is a collection of facts about our problem which we have gained from the questioning in the first 2 steps. This is ***evidence-based*** information.

What I've heard from others
This box of information is made up of things other people have told us about the issue. We need to remember that hearsay or opinion can be subjective, not objective fact. Open to personal bias, this information needs to be treated as ***assumption***.

What I <u>think</u> I know
Testing our evidence-based facts that we know for sure against the things we have heard from others, will give us some answers or suggestions. But, the word 'think' in the statement, tells us this is based on ***assumption***, not fact. We can collect these answers, but they need further scrutiny.

What I need to find out
Having found some answers, we need to check how many of those are based on assumptions and list the things for which we need to find ***evidence-based*** answers to help in our decision making. These then feed back into 'What I <u>know</u> for sure'.

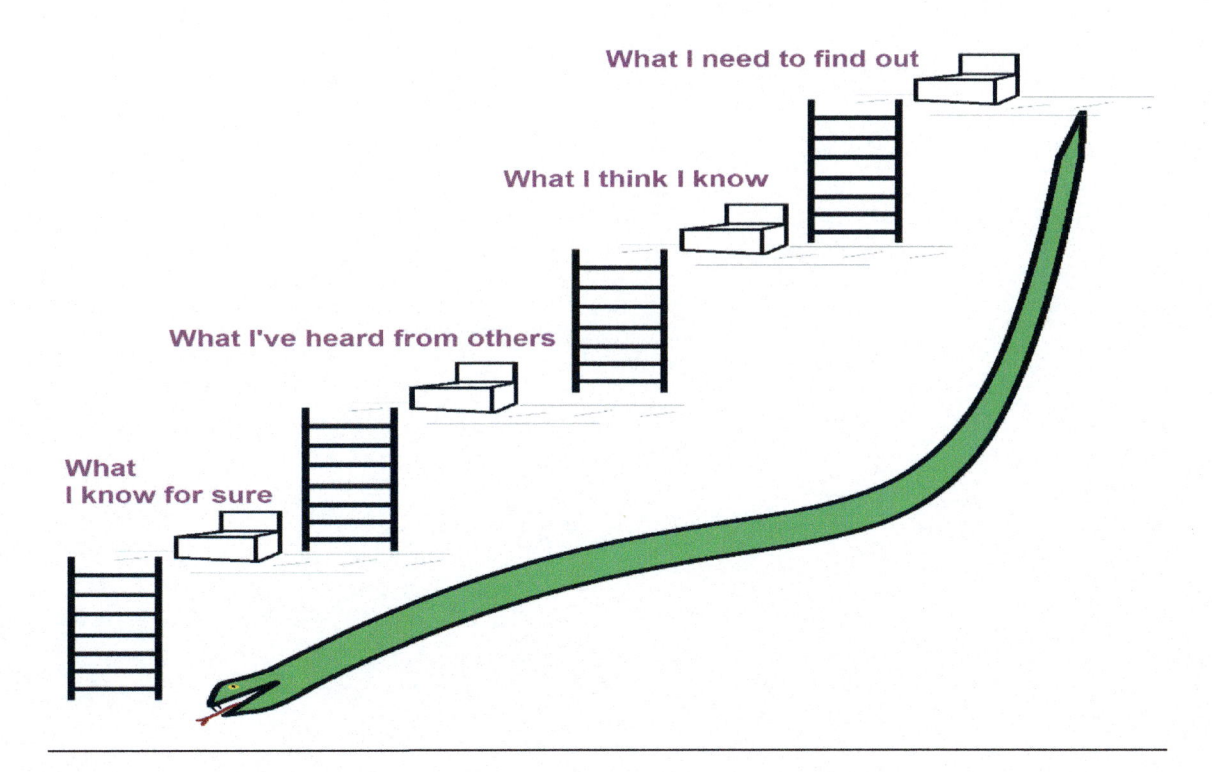

Step 3 summary

Having reached this stage of problem solving, we now have a list of evidence upon which we can start to make decisions. We have search for evidence to separate fact from assumption, found out which aspects need more information and we now have a clear list of what we want and need, in order to help solve the problem.

Our next stage is to find as many different solutions as possible, for which we can use a spider-gram or brainstorming exercise.

Session 5 – The 6 Problem solving steps

Step 4 Solutions

In step 4, we throw caution to the wind and start throwing all sorts of ideas and potential solutions into a Brainstorming or Spider-gram chart. The main aspect to remember here is, it's not actually about the quality of the suggestions, it's more about the quantity. We are not analysing the effectiveness of each suggestion at this point, merely creating a big list of potential solutions, getting as many down as possible. From this exercise, we will apply another tool to check the pros and cons of each suggestion before we decide which will work best for our solution.

Start with a circle in the middle of the page.
This circle should have you in the middle and a short description of the problem.

Start randomly adding single words or very short suggestions around the page, with lines linking you and the problem to each suggestion. It doesn't matter if you are not confident with the validity of the suggestion yet, just get as many down as possible before we move to the next stage.

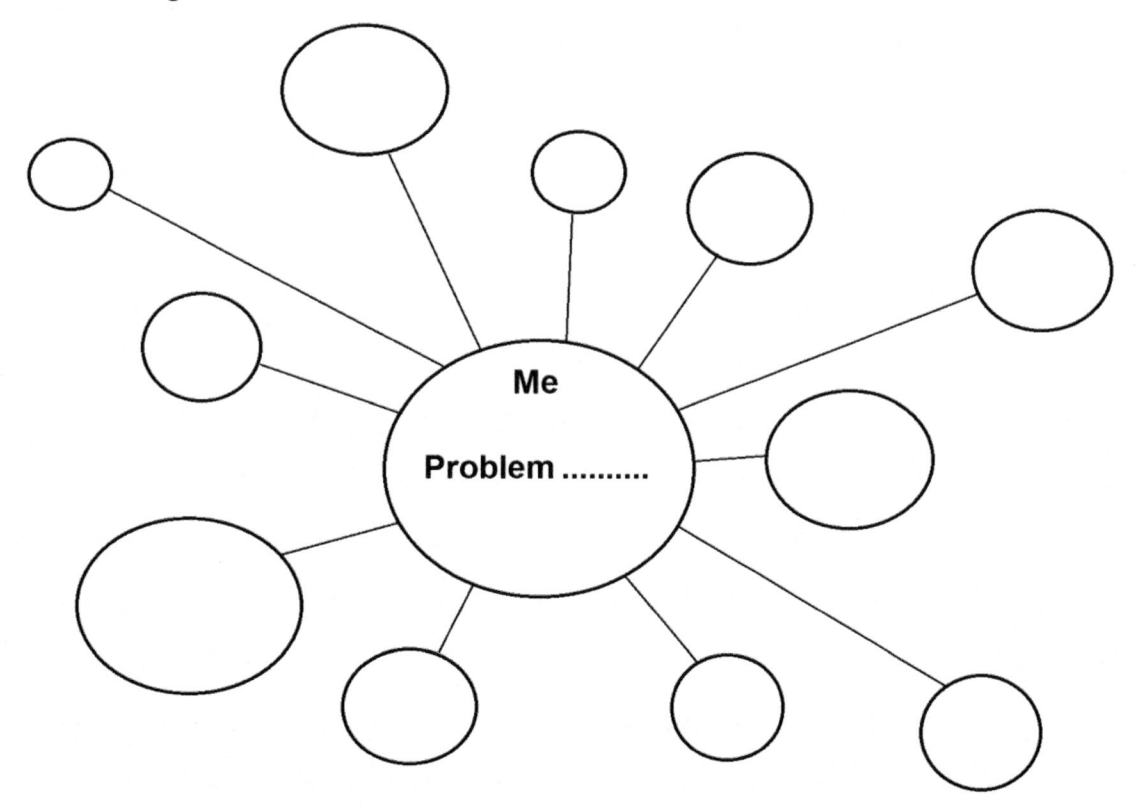

Step 4 summary

The key in this section is to get as many different types of solution / suggestions as possible, without individually assessing each one before you add it to the diagram. This will help us to think in ways which are 'outside the box' or at least be a little freer with our choices and suggestions, rather than relying on ways which have become our standard answers used in the past.

If you find it difficult to come up with different suggestions, speak to someone else and ask them for suggestions. We will do another check on the information we receive for these suggestions in the next step, so, to ensure we don't make any mistakes, we will weigh up these solutions before we commit to making a decision.

Session 6 – The 6 Problem solving steps

Step 5 Weighing solutions

In step 5, we look at all the potential solutions, check which ones appear to be the most likely to work and draw up a shortlist of 2 or 3 that are also in keeping with the things that are most important to us, our personal values. We then draw out expected outcomes from each of these solutions, their pros and cons for both short term and long-term costs and benefits:

- Short-term costs - everything negative about choosing the solution now
- Short-term benefits – everything positive about choosing that solution now
- Long-term costs – everything negatively affected in the future, by that solution
- Long-term benefits – everything positively affected in the future, by that solution

Solution:

Costs	Benefits
Short-term	Short-term
Long-term	Long-term

- Short term benefits with long-term costs = new problems in the future.
- Short-term costs with long-term benefits = requires careful thought, patience & focus
- Short-term costs with long term costs = not a good choice
- Short-term benefits with long-term benefits = the best solution

Goals

Once we start looking at costs and benefits, why we need to do things and how they affect us and those around us, we begin to notice we are creating two types of goals. Those things we want more of and those we want less of in our lives.

- Things we want more of, are called approach goals.
- Things we want less of, are called avoidant goals.

They are both goals and both can help to support our chosen solution, but they can have a different effect on us in terms of our determination to succeed.

Avoidant goals
Can be seen as retreating from something. We can understand this as a defensive manoeuvre. If you give ground too much, stay defensive for too long, be PASSIVE for too long, it can have a detrimental effect on our state of mind and our confidence to succeed. So, even though it's a goal, it can still feel negative.

Approach goals
Things that we actively seek out. We go forward towards them, not retreat from them. They are more positive, making us feel better, going forward not backwards. This is being ASSERTIVE. As they are positive things, we feel a sense of achievement when we attain them, it makes us feel good and gives us the positivity we need to carry on.

Where possible then, we try to focus on and add more approach goals into our plan than avoidant goals, which gives us a more positive feeling to achieving those goals.

Step 5 summary

Once we have completed a short and long-term costs and benefits exercise for each of our most prominent short-listed solutions, we can then choose the best option and begin to make a plan to put that solution into action.

Step 6 is where we think about and create this plan and ensure that we give ourselves achievable and time-sensitive goals to work towards solving our problem.

Session 7 – The 6 Problem solving steps

Step 6 Plan actions

Our last step starts by creating a spider-gram or spider chart. As with the diagram in step 4, draw a circle in the middle of the page with you in the circle and this time leave space to add the option or solution from Step 5 in the bottom half of the same circle. Six lines should emanate from this middle circle, at the end of which, should be another circle (6 in total), each of which, contains one of the following headings:

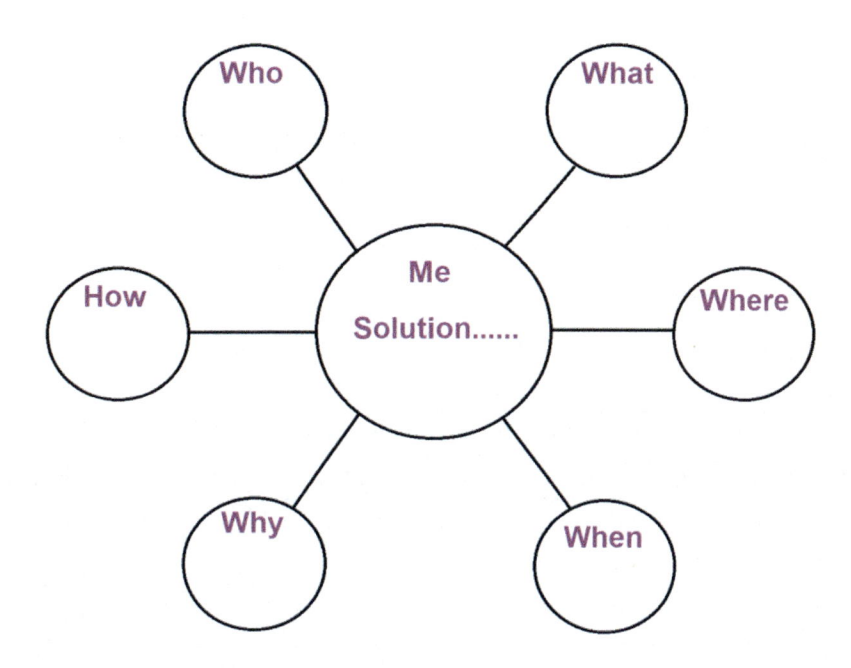

[Spider diagram with central circle labeled "Me Solution......" connected to six outer circles labeled: Who, What, Where, When, Why, How]

Answer the questions in the circles relating to the solution we selected in Step 5:

Who do I need to speak to, to do / ask …… I need to speak to…
What do I need to find out / ask …. I need to ask….
Where do I need to go to get / find out… I need to get……
When is the best time to go to / do / ask …. I need to book time at….
Why is it important to find out / ask / do …. I must remember…
How do I get there / say what I need / find more info …. I also need to know…

These are listed just as an example. Fill these question bubbles with answers specific to your goal and your own Step 5 solution.

Session 8 – The 6 Problem solving steps

Creating a plan of action – mini-actions

We now have a good amount of evidence-based information, a carefully chosen solution to our problem, for which we've weighed up the short and long-term benefits and we have split that solution up via our spider-gram into a list of mini-actions, things we need to do to put that solution into action. Now we need to create a plan of action, to prioritise the order in which we do these things and give ourselves specific and attainable dates by which to achieve them.

To create our check list, we need to write out all the mini-actions and decide on two things:
An order of priority – some things need to be done first, to set up others
Replace as many avoidant goals as possible with approach goals.

Simple example

Problem – Overworked and stressed | **Solution** – I need to book a holiday

1	Who – I need to speak to my boss and ask to book time off	By tomorrow
2	Why – Because I'm feeling stressed and need a break to relax	By tomorrow
3	What – I need to check if someone is already off when I want to go and if cover is available	By tomorrow
4	When – Ask boss to confirm when you're likely to hear back, so I can get on and book a holiday	By tomorrow
5	Where – Go into a travel agent to get them to check all options for the dates I want to go on holiday	Next Saturday
6	How - How am I getting there? What is less stress going to and from the airport? drive, ask a friend or public transport?	Next Saturday

Whether the problem is simple or complex, the same rules to the solution still apply. Have a go at all the steps to problem solving, creating your own check list of mini-actions to support the solution to your problem.

Step 6 summary

Once you are actively solving your problem or achieving your goal, don't forget that re-evaluation is a key aspect of our learning. Check back on what you've done to achieve success and ask yourself questions. Did it resolve as expected? Did it cause any further issues? Did you feel as expected once you solved it? It may be necessary to go back and try one of the other solutions if you didn't get the desired results, but either way, always check back and learn from the process, as this helps us with problem solving in the future.

Problem Solving summary
As you've seen through this section, there's a lot that goes into solving problems. Like going from one side of the pond to the other, there are several steps, but these steps are closely linked. Leaving big gaps between the steps risks falling in, failure. Keeping the steps closely linked, taking information gathered from one to the next one, helps continue to build a secure pathway forward.

Think about what you've learned about yourself and others, through this process. Remember that the keys to solving problems sometimes lay within the attitude or state of mind we are in to begin with. Stress is a massive factor in ill health and has major effects on mental, emotional and physical health. Anything we can do to relieve stress is going to improve our situation, so dealing with problems is far better than trying to avoid them as avoidance just causes more stress. If you find you are avoiding problems, then this gives you an indication that your state of mind or attitude may need adjusting, to enable you to have the focus and drive to achieve your goals.

Avoidant or negative attitudes will hold us back, deplete our confidence and give confidence and free reign to those who would seek to oppress us. As well as using awareness of state of mind and problem-solving skills to enhance our self-confidence, remember that as such, these are also very good self-defence tools. A healthy state of mind is key to a good defence. We must not forget that self-defence is not only defending ourselves from others, it also helps in our defence against the self, which is at the heart of all true Martial Arts.

Learning Styles

When trying to learn the many different aspects of the Mizu Ryu Ju Jutsu syllabus, or indeed, any subject, remember that we all learn in different ways. This is especially important to remember when teaching. We can very easily fall into the trap of using only one method to get information across, but the method of teaching is not a one-size-fits-all situation. Sometimes it is necessary to use more than one method to get information across, to make sure that everyone has a fair chance of understanding the information. As individuals, people find that different methods help that information to sink in more easily, by using different processes to link the observation, understanding, storing and recollection of that information.

As a student, try to identify the learning style which best helps you to understand, retain and recall information. Understanding your own learning style will greatly help you to know how to ask for specific help if the information needs to be delivered in a different way. This is understanding how you best learn and is key to success in every field of learning, not just Martial Arts. Whoever teaches you will understand about different learning styles, but in a class environment, it may take some time to figure out the individual styles of everyone, so, if you can identify yours for yourself, you can meet the instructor half-way. Structuring your questions in a way which works best for you, helps you learn more quickly, and the instructor can be more mindful of your learning style, more efficient and helpful when teaching.

There are 4 main learning styles as defined by Neil Fleming's VARK model in 1987. Most people will identify strongly with one, but it is also true that most people are a mixture of several, with one being the main learning style which suits you the best. When reading the different styles, which one best suits how you take on board new ideas and information?

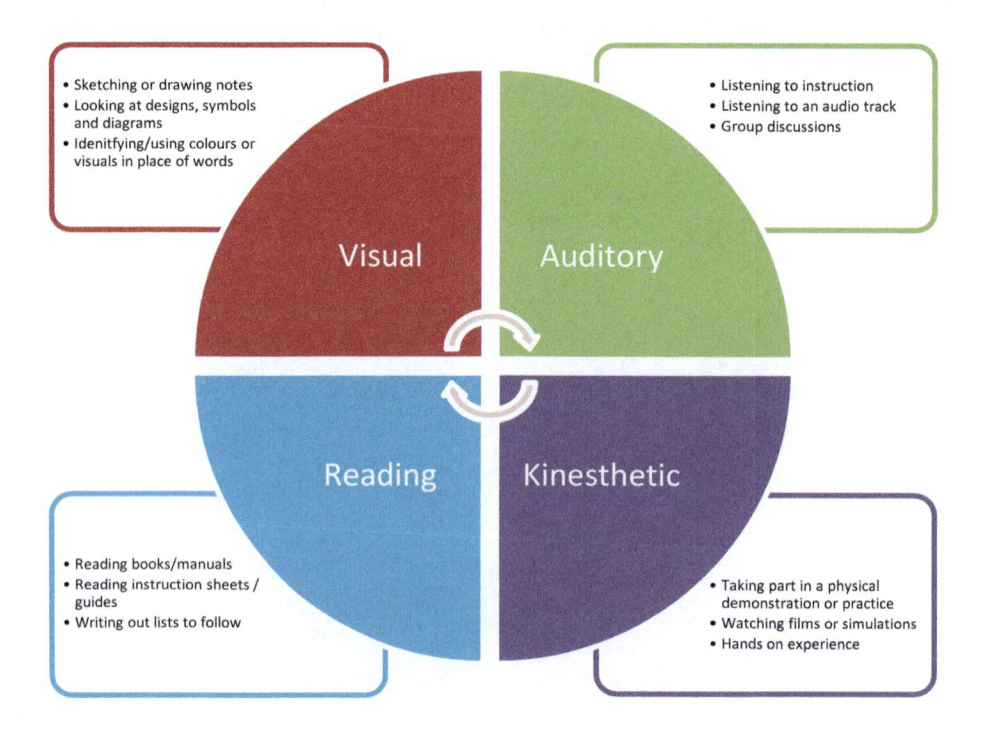

Visual
- Sketching or drawing notes
- Looking at designs, symbols and diagrams
- Identifying/using colours or visuals in place of words

Auditory
- Listening to instruction
- Listening to an audio track
- Group discussions

Reading
- Reading books/manuals
- Reading instruction sheets / guides
- Writing out lists to follow

Kinesthetic
- Taking part in a physical demonstration or practice
- Watching films or simulations
- Hands on experience

Autism

Most of you will be aware that we are an autism friendly club and that we are proud to support Fighting For Autism Charity. As an affiliate club, recognised by the charity, we support the charity's aims for providing equality of training opportunities for everyone and information for those wishing to understand more about what autism is and how they can help support others on the autistic spectrum.

From the NHS Website:
'Being autistic does not mean you have an illness or disease. It means your brain works in a different way from other people…
Autism is not a medical condition with treatments or a cure. But some people need support to help them with certain things…
Autism is a spectrum. This means everybody with autism is different…some autistic people need little or no help, others may need help from a parent or carer every day.'

Autism has been known by different names over the years, including:
- Autism Spectrum Disorder (ASD)
- Autism Spectrum Condition (ASC)
- Asperger's or Asperger Syndrome.

Sometimes, people with autism also have one or more other conditions such as *dyslexia, dyspraxia, anxiety, depression, ADHD, epilepsy and Savant syndrome*. It is not caused by bad parenting, vaccines, diet or infection. We talk about autism regularly at the club, but the best way to get the basics covered in this manual without going into too much detail, is to simply provide you with a copy of the Autism 101 fact sheets provided by Fighting For Autism. We have had members in the club who are diagnosed as on the autistic spectrum, those who are undiagnosed and those who support people on the spectrum at school or in their home life.

Our Chief Instructor is a Trustee and Charity Secretary for the Fighting For Autism (Europe) Charity, so for any further information, either speak to Tony Sensei or you can contact the charity directly

Website www.fightingforautismeurope.org.uk

Email info@fightingforautismeurope.org.uk

As we are all about learning and education at this club, for a more in depth understanding about autism, you can sign up to do a free online course by Open University on their Open Learning Platform. It is a very good course and quite detailed.
Understanding autism - OpenLearn - Open University

FIGHTING FOR AUTISM

www.fightingforautismeurope.org.uk

PAGE 1

UNDERSTANDING AUTISM FOR KIDS

CREATING AWARENESS & ACCEPTANCE FOR A BETTER QUALITY OF LIFE!

AUTISM 101 FOR KIDS

WHAT IS AUTISM?

Autism affects the way a person's body and brain work together. People with Autism may have trouble following directions, making new friends, talking to people and listening sometimes. You can't "catch it" and you might not know if someone has Autism. Kids with Autism might have trouble in school.

Kids with Autism are just as cool as you are!

UNDERSTANDING AUTISM
EVERYONE IS EQUAL. AUTISM DOES NOT MEAN LESS.

Kids with Autism may have some trouble at school with listening, following directions, and communicating. They might be quiet or they could be loud at times. With the help of teachers and friends who care, family, and classmates, kids with Autism can have an easier time.

Sometimes, kids with Autism are misunderstood and have trouble playing with other kids. Because of this, some kids tease, pick on, and bully them. It is important to never treat anyone mean or badly because they are different.

Some kids with Autism may act differently and might do some unusual things. Some may have trouble with certain activities, but really be great at others. Everyone with Autism is unique.

Talking, listening, and communicating can be hard at times for kids with Autism. Be patient. Be understanding. Be a good friend. They might just need a little extra time to put their thoughts into words. They aren't ingoring you.

Some kids with Autism prefer that schedules stay the same or that people always sit in the same seats. They may have a tough time when things change, so they may try telling people what to do or where to sit. Just know that they aren't being trying to be bossy, just getting used to change so they know what's coming next and don't get upset.

DARE TO BE DIFFERENT

FIGHTING FOR AUTISM

www.fightingforautismeurope.org.uk

PAGE 2

UNDERSTANDING AUTISM *FOR KIDS*

CREATING AWARENESS & ACCEPTANCE FOR A BETTER QUALITY OF LIFE!

AUTISM 101 FOR KIDS

WHAT CAUSES AUTISM?

Doctors, Scientists and other Researchers don't know what exactly causes people to be born with Autism.

In Europe 1 in 89 people live with a diagnosis of Autism.

Autism is much more common in boys than in girls.

There is no medical test to diagnose Autism and currently no known "cure" for Autism.

SOME KIDS WITH AUTISM MIGHT:
SOME THINGS YOU MIGHT SEE KIDS WITH AUTISM DO.

- Have trouble talking, make strange sounds or noises, or not talk at all.
- Flap their hands, rock, spin, laugh a lot, or may get upset.
- Sit quietly and not look at others.
- Choose to play alone and not interact with others.
- Play or behave differently than other classmates.
- Be very active and have lots of energy.
- Have trouble looking directly at you, or respond when you talk to them
- Do or say the same things over and over again.

WHY DO KIDS WITH AUTISM ACT THIS WAY?

Some kids with Autism don't see, hear, or feel things the same way we do. For instance, the sound of the school bell or the noise of a parade may hurt their ears. Some may have trouble eating certain foods because of the way they taste or feel in their mouth. Others may smell things differently, and smells we usually like, such as cookies, may make them feel sick. And, things that hurt us, may not be painful to them.

It can be hard for kids with Autism to understand what we say or what our expressions mean. Sometimes, showing a picture may help your classmate understand what you are talking about. The best thing you can do is to be friendly and to help them fit in with everyone else.

YOU NEVER KNOW WHO HAS AUTISM. IT'S BEST TO JUST BE NICE!

FIGHTING FOR AUTISM

www.fightingforautismeurope.org.uk

PAGE 3

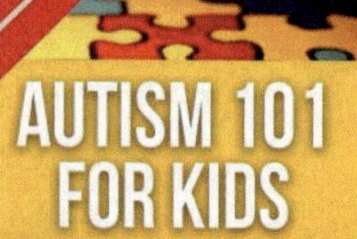

UNDERSTANDING AUTISM FOR KIDS

CREATING AWARENESS & ACCEPTANCE FOR A BETTER QUALITY OF LIFE!

AUTISM 101 FOR KIDS

AUTISM IN SCHOOL

Kids with Autism can be in many different types of classrooms and schools. They may be a member of your class or may be in a classroom that was set up especially for them. Many kids with Autism also participate in after-school activities with classmates, friends, and neighbors. You may see a special aid with someone with Autism helping them have the best school day they can.

"YOU CAN MAKE A GREAT NEW FRIEND IF YOU ARE ALWAYS ACCEPTING"

HOW CAN I BECOME FRIENDS WITH SOMEONE WHO HAS AUTISM?

- You are on the right track by taking time to learn what Autism is. Understanding and accepting people with Autism is the best first step to becoming friends with someone who has Autism.
- Always accept your friend for who they are. We are all different from each other. Never try to change someone.
- Know that some kids with Autism are really smart, just in a different way.
- Talk in smaller sentences with simple words and use gestures like pointing, use pictures, write down what you want to say to help your friend understand.
- Join your new friend in activities that interest him or her, and invite them to join in on activities you like to do. Just be sure to be nice if they don't want to play at times.
- Be patient and know that your friend doesn't mean to bother you or others.
- Teach your other friends about Autism and include your new friend with your other frinds.
- Be a leader. You can teach your friend a lot, and they may look up to you for showing them that you are nice and care about them.

IF YOU WANT TO KNOW MORE ABOUT AUTISM. ASK A TEACHER.

FIGHTING FOR AUTISM

www.fightingforautismeurope.org.uk

PAGE 4

UNDERSTANDING AUTISM *FOR KIDS*

CREATING AWARENESS & ACCEPTANCE FOR A BETTER QUALITY OF LIFE!

AUTISM 101 FOR KIDS

WHAT IS FIGHTING FOR AUTISM? HOW CAN I FOLLOW THEM?
ARE YOU A MMA, MUAY THAI, BOXING, JIU-JITSU, OR WRESTLING FAN? FOLLOW US ONLINE!

Fighting for Autism is an Autism Awareness & Advocacy Charitable Organization. We have Operations in Australia, Europe and the USA.

We promote our various Programs & Initiatives primarily through the fight industry, such as MMA, Muay Thai, Boxing, Jiu-Jitsu and Pro Wrestling. Follow us online to learn more.

Some of our Programs & Initiatives Include:

- Fighter Ambassador Program/Mentor Program
- Junior Ambassador and Club affiliate Program
- Autism Education Program
- Anti-Bullying Initiative
- Technology Initiative
- Awareness, Acceptance and Inclusion Initiatives
- Adaptive Athletics Inclusion Program

WANT TO LEARN MORE ABOUT AUTISM?
LOOK FOR THESE BOOKS AT YOUR LIBRARY OR ONLINE!

Amenta, C. (1992). Russell is extra special: A book about autism for children New York, NY: Magination Press

Bishop, B. (2002). My friend with autism. Arlington, TX: Future Horizons, Inc.

Bleach, F. (2001). Everybody is different: A book for young people who have brothers or sisters with autism. Shawnee Mission, KS: Autism Asperger Publishing Company.

Edwards, A. (2001). Taking autism to school. Plainview, NY: JayJo Books, LLC.

Keating-Velasco, J. (2007). A is for autism, F is for friend. Shawnee Mission, KS: Autism Asperger Publishing Company

Lowell, J. & Tuchel, T. (2005). My best friend Will. Shawnee Mission, KS: Autism Asperger Publishing Company

TOGETHER WE CAN CHANGE THE WORLD FOR THE BETTER!

Mental Training

In traditional Japanese martial training, there are three stages to attack awareness that are fundamentally important to kata, and to the understanding and application of the techniques within a particular school.

The Three Attacks

- **Go no sen** meaning 'after' or 'late' attack. This involves a counter technique in response to an attack i.e. the attack happens, it fails or you block/redirect and then you reply with a counter technique. It can also be when you deliberately use a technique to create an opening as your opponent blocks it, to then exploit that opening for your 'after' attack.
- **Sen no sen** is when you launch a technique simultaneously with the attack of the opponent i.e. the opponent has chosen what they are going to do, facial and body cues make you aware of the imminent attack and you act immediately at the same time as them, to not be caught out.
- **Sensen no sen** is a technique launched in anticipation of an attack. It is where the opponent has decided what to do, is fully committed to their attack, psychologically and physically beyond the point of no return. Importantly, having analysed and understood the intention and available or likely outcomes, the timing is such that you act even before the opponent has initiated their attack i.e. 'sensing' that an attack is imminent and what that attack is going to be, and acting before it has started.

In very basic terms, we could succinctly characterise the 3 attacks as:
- Go no sen - exploiting a gap in the opponent's defences.
- Sen no sen - beating them to the draw.
- Sensen no sen - Pre-emptive striking.

The term Pre-emptive striking gives some clue to understanding the principle of Sensen no sen, but it is too simplistic. Sensen no sen involves a timing and technique choice born from an analysis of the opponent, their thoughts, intentions and technique range, rather than just simply 'getting the first one in'.

3 Personal Examples – Go no sen? Sen no Sen? Sensen no sen? Luck?

Shopping
As an adult, I was shopping in a supermarket, walking down an isle. At the other end of the isle, I could see a mother with her child in hand, walking on the right side of the isle, towards me. The boy must have only been about 7 years old. Even though there was around 10-12 feet between us, I could 'sense' that this little boy was going to do something to me when close enough. His anger, hatred, whatever it was, was that strong, I could sense the intent of his thoughts towards me. As we drew closer, I took a Tsuri Ashi step to my left and the timing was such that, not knowing I had anticipated his attack, he committed to barging into me with his right shoulder, only to find, I wasn't there anymore! The fact that I wasn't there for him to barge into, meant that, having committed himself to that physical act, he had nothing physical to contact and he fell into the space and ended up on the floor. His mother, unaware of his thoughts or the situation, assumed he had tripped over his own feet, or hers

and asked if he was alright. I looked at him on the floor, astounded that such anger could reside in such a young person. He looked up at me not fully understanding how his attack had failed and saw my disapproving glare, staring back down at him.

Walking Home
I was aged 15, walking home from town, through an area known as having a violent rivalry between the teenagers here and where I lived. I noticed some 'gang members' playing football on a grass area to the right of the path I was on. I knew it would have been obvious that I was from the 'rival estate' so, seemingly ignoring them, but being very vigilant, I continued walking on the path, look straight ahead. I 'became aware' that one of them had kicked the ball directly at me. Outside of my peripheral vision, approximately at the 4 o'clock position, I thought it was speeding towards my head. Rather than put my hands up to block, or looking round, I stopped. The ball flew straight past my face. I then took one extra big step forward. The ball bounced off the lamppost to my front left and rebounded past the back of my head, back towards the grassy area. Without so much as a flinch or looking round, I continued walking on the path. I could tell that all those on the grass were just standing staring. No other attempt towards me was made then, or at any other time after that.

Another Skinhead encounter
Aged 13, I was walking with a friend of mine after school, towards his house. We were mucking around, general 'horseplay' and oblivious of anyone else around. Suddenly, a Skinhead, decked in stereotypical shaved head, bleached jeans, red braces, Fred Perry polo shirt, doc martens and national front tattoos, grabbed me and tried to push me towards a nearby fence. He was around 17 years old. Older, taller and stronger, he had a significant advantage as he initiated contact before I was aware. As I took a step back, I grabbed him and threw him towards the fence, with Tai Otoshi. Circling round, with my right shoulder facing the fence, he got up and launched a kind of roundhouse kick/Mawashi Geri to my left side with his right foot. Knowing he had steel plated boots on, I absolutely did not want to be hit by that. I caught the kick with my left arm, whilst moving diagonally to my right. Still holding his leg, I threw him with Ashi Mochi / O Uchi Gari. He landed (thankfully) flat on his back, not on his head. My friend was shouting at this point, telling the guy to stop. When he got back up he came close to grab but there was no intention to attack. I had also grabbed him in preparation, but it was obvious at that point he'd already been embarrassed by being thrown around by a 'kid' and just wanted a way to back down and save face. He said he thought I was attacking someone and therefore, he jumped in to save my friend....this gave him his out, as, after reassurance that we were both friends and there was no need for 'intervention', he retreated and we went on our way.

Can you identify any of the 3 attack principles?
There are many more anecdotes I could choose from. Of these 3 different examples of being attacked, only one resulted in physically combative responses from me.
Use these to stimulate your own thoughts.
Was I right?
Was I wrong?
How would you react in the same situations?

Martial states of mind

We have covered some states of mind information in the Problem-Solving Tools section, when we looked at common aspects of Passive, Aggressive, Passive-aggressive and Assertive states of mind. In traditional Japanese Martial Arts, there are several 'states of mind' referred to, which have other, wider implications, that obviously originate from more Eastern influence and understanding. Some basic explanations follow, but more should be learned by further discussion and research.

Shoshin

Often referred to as 'Beginners mind' is not a derogatory term by any means. In fact, attaining Shoshin, is actually quite difficult for someone who has been learning for some time. We easily forget what it was like for us as a beginner because we have made personal improvements in both application and understanding. But, true adepts will understand there is unpredictability, openness and innocence where beginners are concerned. In physical aspects, beginners aren't aware of or haven't fully adopted the 'rules', so will often think or act in ways not expected. Secondarily, the simplicity and awe with which the beginner sees the world, can diminish over time with overexposure and complacency. At the same time, the openness that a beginner has to learning new things and accepting information, is often lost by those who, after training for some time, mistakenly believe they have all the answers. A very well-known Martial Arts instructor in the UK once told me, he learned everything about Ju Jutsu in 5 years and after 10 years there was nothing new for him to learn! Humility perhaps? To surround yourself with people other than sycophants? Shoshin is a Zen concept of looking at the world with the beginner's mind. No preconceptions, rooted in the present, open and eager to learn. Shoshin, is a form of mindfulness.

Fudoshin

We cover a few aspects of Fudo Myo-o, earlier in the book on p92. Fudoshin is to embody those aspects of Fudo Myo-o in our thoughts, actions and deeds. As Fudo Myo-o is known as 'The immovable one' Fudoshin can be said to be a mindset that ensures steadfastness in your thoughts and decisions, not being easily swayed by barriers, failure or self-doubt, and keeping true to your goals and intentions. Immovable as a mountain (hence Fudo Myo-o being depicted stood or sat on a boulder) Fudoshin also links to the strength of mind to carry through the purpose of one's thoughts and actions. Another short description of Fudoshin is your reflection in water. When you look into it, the water reflects your image instantly and unchanged. Throw a stone onto the water and the ripples distort the image and you lose sight of it. If you wait, once the ripples have subsided, the water stills and your image is reflected, as unchanged as before. Fudoshin, then, has commonality with perseverance, falls just short of stubbornness and so, draws close to my favourite self-description of 'Persistently determined'.

Zanshin

Essentially, Zanshin is described as: 'a constant state of relaxed alertness'.

It is the state within which your vigilance is heightened, especially after a recent conflict, but it is not interfering with your ability to continue your duties. For a more comprehensive explanation of Zanshin, see the article written on page 136, along with the accompanying concepts of Zenshin and Tsushin.

Mushin

Mushin or 'no mindedness' or 'empty mind' is easily misunderstood as not thinking of anything. I remember the words of my Reiki Grandmaster, Taggart King:

'Mushin is not simply thinking of nothing, as, thinking of nothing, is still thinking of something. Or rather, thinking about thinking of nothing'.

Mushin is to empty the mind of the emotions, preconceived ideas and actions that could be temporarily stored in the forefront of your mind, as a precursor to a decision to act. Mushin is an intuitive mindset, deciding to allow your body and your instincts to act instantly, without processing chains of thoughts which might slow the process of instinctive and intuitive action. In another explanation, Mushin could be said to be the state where the mind, rather than being switched off, is actually working at very high speeds of analysis, but with no specific plan or direction of intention as the emotions and plans of action have been excluded from the current analysis. This brings about a more Zen-like attitude towards the situation, dispensing with preconceived ideas and aids in a more fluent response to the situation.

Personal Experience

In all the fights I've been involved in over the years in my job as a Head Doorman, the vast majority of the time, I have unconsciously adopted Mushin more times than any other mindset. Sometimes you have a specific action to target, like 'He has a bottle in his hand and he's coming towards me' but, oftentimes, you don't know what's going to happen, so you have to rid yourself of a preconceived action plan and react intuitively to what you feel is going to happen, when it happens. You start with the most immediate threat, then allow your instincts and body to choose the next action. This is reinforced by your training, ensuring you have chains of action stored in instantly recallable movement, that actually work. Experience is added into the mix during this process of analysis, but it's not easy to do, especially under the threat of real violence. Our instincts can be overruled by our response to our emotions and our adrenal system when the fight, flight or freeze syndrome kicks into place. We also need to maintain emotional control to not go overboard in our responses. That's why it's important to adopt Mushin to eradicate the negative emotions which might endanger you by playing into self-doubt and fear. You still experience fear, but you recognise and use it as a response to your adrenaline, powering your rection to the situation and keeping yourself or others safe.

Intent

We speak often of intent, the mindset, decision and determination to achieve a goal. Intent is a massive part of Reiki and Martial Arts, in both action and non-action, deciding whether to do, or not do something, as well as the level at which that action should be pitched.

Throwing a punch at a pad without intent, is the same as saying sorry to someone without really meaning it. It is empty, meaningless and does not achieve the goal you set out to achieve. Merely going through the motions is a futile waste of time and energy. When you do something, use the correct intent and you will have far more chance of achieving your goal.

An athlete uses aggression to embolden their performance, but it doesn't mean they are an aggressive person. The intent used to achieve the goal ensures more effort and focus is applied to that goal. So, if you have to apologise to someone, apologise with intent. If you have to hit someone to defend yourself or others, hit with intent. If you reach the **Red** state of mind and are actively engaged in fight or flight, you must fully understand and feel that it is an emergency situation. Your health and well-being, or that of family or friends is at risk.

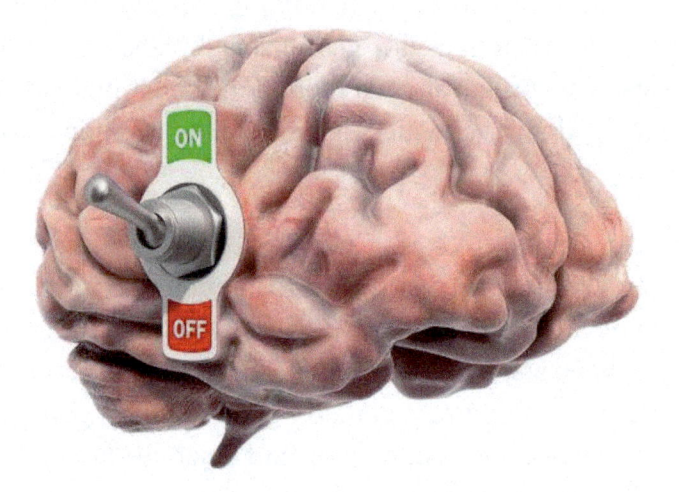

Finding the Switch
It takes time, effort, visualisation and practice, to find that switch inside your head – the one that, once on, turns you into an utter nightmare. We are all capable of great violence. It is our character, our morality, our integrity, which stops us from misusing that power, using it only when necessary.

The problem at first, is fighting that compassionate side of ourselves, to get access to that switch. Most of us are compassionate people and even if we are practicing a technique, there is a conversation going on in our head which tells us not to cause harm. We need to be able to take control of that voice, know where the switch is and be able to flip it at the right time, for the right reasons, because, what will happen if we don't step up? Who will defend us or our families? Sometimes you need to act and hesitation may take that choice away from you.

Flipping the switch
The next problem for some is, once they flip that switch, they find it difficult to switch it back off again. This again comes down to emotional awareness, recognising cues and understanding when to stop. There are moral and legal ramifications for getting it wrong!

A true martial artist has their finger hovering next to that switch all the time and they can switch it on and off, at will, anytime it is required.

The fictional Marvel character Bruce Banner, sums this up nicely, in the MCU film, The Avengers (2012). Faced with a massive onslaught of aliens trying to wipe out everyone on planet Earth, Captain America says to Banner 'Now might be a good time to get angry' The calm and as yet untransformed Banner replies, 'That's my secret Cap, I'm always angry' and instantly transforms into the Hulk to deliver a punch to a gigantic alien. As a perfect link to what I'm talking about, the previous Hulk film, sees Banner learning to control his anger by going to Brazil to learn Jiu Jitsu from Rickson Gracie. Thus, having learned to control his rage without deleting it, he was able to instantly switch it on or off, whenever it was needed.

Superhuman Strength
Real-life examples like Angela Cavallo, a mother who lifts the car off her trapped son with her bare hands, or Lauren Kornacki, a 22-year-old woman who similarly raised a BMW 525i off her father when the car toppled from a jack, show that the 'Superhuman' ability is already within us. It just needs the right motivation and intent to access it. Scientifically, it's called 'Hysterical Strength' Scientists know it's there, they just don't know how we access it.

Intent though, is more than just anger, or the ability to use aggression when needed. Intent is at the heart of everything we do in Martial Arts and Reiki. It can be a massive positive factor in achieving our goals and the power it releases in us, should never be underestimated.

Zanshin – The footpath analogy

In the western world of Japanese Martial Arts (Yes, I'm aware of the oxymoron!), you'll occasionally come across someone talking of Zanshin. Usually there is a short explanation of some mystical power of foresight or reacting so quickly that you had read the mind of the other person, or walking around like a paranoid Ninja expecting people to jump out at you at any minute.

Some explanations seem to be mixed with the concept of **Haragei,** being in tune with and acting upon our gut feeling or intuition. All are somewhat related to 3 different aspects of mental awareness, of which **Zanshin** is one: **Zenshin, Tsushin** & **Zanshin**.

To explain what each one represents in a simple and relatable way, let's use the 3-part example of walking to the shops along a public footpath.

Part 1. You are out, walking down a public path towards the shops. Having listened in your lessons, you are in the 'Yellow' mindset: relaxed, but aware. You are concentrating on where you are going, but also noticing other people and obstacles around you, even though you know the route very well. You see a potential problem ahead of you, maybe a manhole cover not in place, or someone who's just exited their house, got in their car and who might reverse into your path if they are not paying attention. You become mindful of the potential obstacles, preparing yourself to act if necessary.

> *1.1 This is Zenshin – Relaxed yet aware of any possible danger. Sending your mind forward, ahead of your physical form, to ascertain information about hazards and risks in the environment. Situational awareness like this, allows you to read ahead and act thoughtfully, if necessary, rather than relying solely on impulsive decisions and reactions. In modern risk assessment analysis, Zenshin would be the first 2 aspects; Identify the hazard and Assess the risk (the likelihood of the hazard causing harm).*

Part 2. As you get closer to the house, suddenly, the car pulls out of the driveway in front of you. The driver hasn't seen you. You have already assessed the situation and take action to avoid it. You are using the situational awareness that your *Zenshin* afforded you, to make sure you don't put yourself in any further danger i.e. jumping into the road to avoid it, only to run into the path of another oncoming vehicle, or jumping to the wrong side and falling down the open manhole. You make decisions and judgements about what's happening, and you take action to get out of the way. Your action is based on the previously gained information, as well as details about the situation right now, in case some details have changed since you first assessed the risk. Having made a decision, you focus and commit to an action which will make you evade, minimise, control or remove the threat in front of you.

> *2.1 This is Tsushin - To be actively dealing with the problem, totally committed and focused on the action, based on your informed and thoughtful decision. Tsushin concentrates on the 2 aspects of: Dynamic risk assessment (further assessment after contact with the hazard) and applying Control measures to deal with the hazard.*

Part 3. The car has come to a stop. The driver apologises as they only saw you after you moved out of the way. You look around to check you are OK, that there is no further threat to yourself or others. You check that it is safe to continue whilst maintaining awareness and focus for signs of another threat, either from the same source or a different one.

> *3.1 This is Zanshin - To be aware of any further threat after an encounter. To take a breath, but maintain a 'heightened state of relaxed alertness', ready for another encounter, should there be one. We now come full circle in our risk assessment as Zanshin concentrates on the Review stage, to evaluate actions and decisions, learn from the results and prepare for the future.*

These concepts can have more detailed descriptions, but this simple footpath example, should make for a good foundation from which you can look for more answers.

Hierarchy of Controls

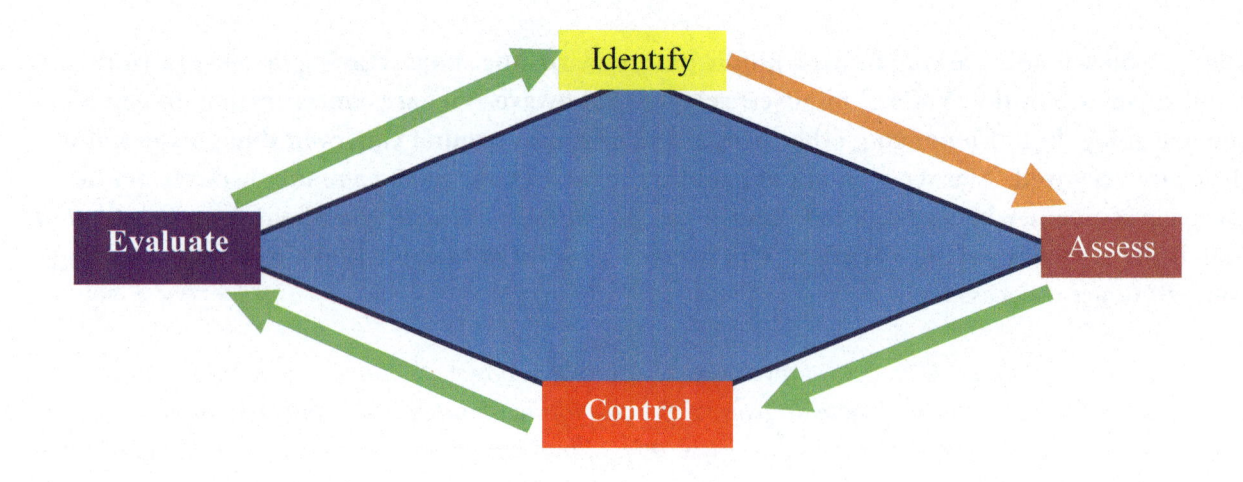

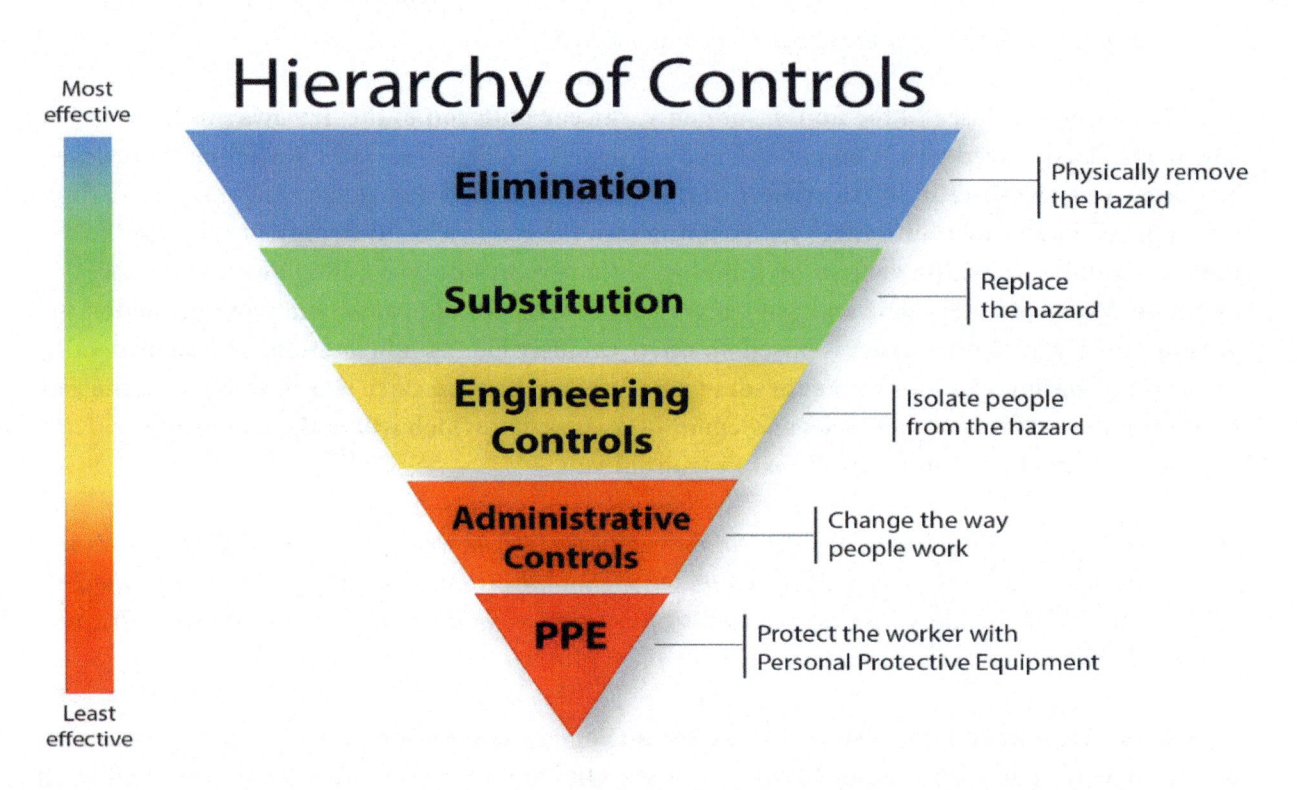

- **Elimination** — Physically remove the hazard
- **Substitution** — Replace the hazard
- **Engineering Controls** — Isolate people from the hazard
- **Administrative Controls** — Change the way people work
- **PPE** — Protect the worker with Personal Protective Equipment

Most effective → Least effective

In our current climate of technological advancement, mobile phones and earbuds are increasingly divorcing us from connecting with our surroundings. Putting yourself in the shoes of our subject walking to the shop, this example shows how important it is to be aware of your surroundings and to look ahead, sometimes quite literally, to be aware of potential problems. Those of you who have read or learned about the Cooper Colour Code and how it relates to our daily mindset, will see that being in the 'White' state of mind rather than 'Yellow' during the walk to the shops, would have led to vastly different consequences with potentially serious injuries.

Much can be gleaned from taking ***Zenshin, Tsushin*** and ***Zanshin*** and developing each one of them within your practice to fully understand their application. Like many other oral explanations in our syllabus, the meaning is not solely attributed to our physical techniques. Adoption of this situationally aware mindset should be maintained for everyday life.

As ever, question, research and discuss.

Masakatsu Agatsu

True Victory is victory over oneself

An article written by Tony Bailey for Martial Arts Guardian Magazine

The Nippon Budōkan, Tōkyo

In the Japanese systems, there are 2 similarly sounding terms which differentiate between the old fighting systems and the newer sport orientated systems - Bujutsu and Budō. Most people are aware that in very simple Japanese, Bu is war and Jutsu is traditional art or techniques. Dō also translated as Michi, is a path or way to follow. A set of teachings you follow which affect the whole lifestyle you live.

Bujutsu

Bujutsu can be further defined as a system of traditionally proved techniques that are practiced in the manner in which they were first founded. Within the fighting world this was the actual techniques used in real hand-to-hand combat in life-or-death situations on the battlefield.

Budō, is creating a life-path to follow for the individual. In the fighting arts, adding those traditional techniques to a training system meant to unify mind, body and spirit. This was for the good of the individual and as a consequence, for the mutual benefit of the community in which he lives and serves as a useful member of society.

Budō

Budō is the way followed by Jūdō, Kendō, Kyūdō, Sūmō, Karatedō, Aikidō, Shorinji Kempō, Naginatadō, and Jūkendō; the collective member sports of the Japanese Budō Association. It is largely associated with an old Japanese maxim:

Masakatsu Agatsu (True Victory, is victory over oneself).

In 1987, at the Budōkan, Tōkyo (which was specifically built to promote Japanese Budō), The Japanese Budō Association formalized The Budō Charter to solidify the philosophy, purpose, structure and aims of Budō training in Japan, with the hope of improving and spreading them throughout the world.

One thing all the member arts have in common, is they all agreed with using the physical techniques of old, with a philosophy and mental training which prepared the individual for the rigors of the modern world. One of the main ways of achieving this was the development of a competitive sport side of training to help this unification process.

The Budō Charter situated at The Budōkan

ARTICLE 1: OBJECTIVE OF BUDŌ

Through physical and mental training in the Japanese martial ways, budō exponents seek to build their character, enhance their sense of judgement, and become disciplined individuals capable of making contributions to society at large.

ARTICLE 2: KEIKO (Training)

When training in budō, practitioners must always act with respect and courtesy, adhere to the prescribed fundamentals of the art, and resist the temptation to pursue mere technical skill rather than strive towards the perfect unity of mind, body and technique.

ARTICLE 3: SHIAI (Competition)

Whether competing in a match or doing set forms (kata), exponents must externalise the spirit underlying budō. They must do their best at all times, winning with modesty, accepting defeat gracefully, and constantly exhibiting self-control.

ARTICLE 4: DŌJŌ (Training Hall)

The dōjō is a special place for training the mind and body. In the dōjō, budō practitioners must maintain discipline, and show proper courtesies and respect.
The dōjō should be a quiet, clean, safe, and solemn environment.

ARTICLE 5: TEACHING

Teachers of budō should always encourage others to also strive to better themselves and diligently train their minds and bodies, while continuing to further their understanding of the technical principles of budō. Teachers should not allow focus to be put on winning or losing in competition, or on technical ability alone. Above all, teachers have a responsibility to set an example as role models.

ARTICLE 6: PROMOTING BUDŌ

Persons promoting budō must maintain an open-minded and international perspective as they uphold traditional values. They should make efforts to contribute to research and teaching, and do their utmost to advance budō in every way.

As I say to my own students:

'Budō is a spiritual journey of self-discovery, through physical means.'

The difficulties you go through in the physical techniques, helping to strengthen your mind and polish your spirit, help to strengthen your resolve to overcome difficulties you come across in other areas of life. Not a new concept as Bodhidharma's teachings at the Shaolin temple during the 5th century, were said to be along these lines. Many Koryu systems eventually arrived at a similar understanding, changing perspective from kill or be killed Bujutsu to Budō. Since this introduction in modern Japan, the various Budō schools have flourished to the point of completely outshining the older Bujutsu arts they originated from.

It is disciplined training which promotes etiquette, skilful technique, physical strength, and the unity of mind and body, which turns those external arts into an internal search for perfection. Mars – the God of War, was also the guardian of agriculture. It is also said that he sought War only to restore peace, so, there's more than one facet to his character and with the aspects being so different; Fighting and agriculture, War and Peace, it reminds us to be multidimensional with a view to our own training in this modern-day era.

As Western esotericism teaches, As above, so below. The microcosm is as the macrocosm. The lessons we learn in the dojo, are there to be equally applied outside it.

Inspired to take his teaching of mutual prosperity, born from his vision for Budō helping to change the world, Jigoro Kano – founder of Judō, addressed the Inter-Parliamentary Union in 1933 with the following:

'The Spirit of mutual prosperity must be respected between nations. With regard to international federations as well, if countries only consider their own gain and disregard other countries, they cannot achieve their true goals. Each country must make it a principle to promote mutual prosperity and must conduct itself with the determination to do its utmost for the world.'

Just let that sink in for a moment. Here was a Japanese man, in the 1930's, telling the world's leaders that they needed to work together for the benefit of ALL countries, not just selfishly looking after their own interests…… and this was 12 years before the UN was founded. Kano Shihan had lofty ideals for the spread of Budō and its principles.

Me and a student of mine at Kano's statue outside the Kodokan 2001

The lesson of Masakatsu Agatsu is very much evident in what Kano was promoting.

When you work through adversity, focus on your goals and strive for personal perfection, whether you achieve it or not, it changes and strengthens you. Through this you are able to resolve many conflicts through perseverance and strategy and have a more peaceful outlook. When you are at peace within yourself, communication and peace with others is far easier to achieve. When you are on this path, you become more serviceable to your family, friends and the community within which you reside as well as having the ability to be able to physically defend those precious things should the need arise, because of your love for them.

I think that is a huge part of why Budō should still be such an important part of training in the 21st Century. I think most of those that belittle the pyjama clad Budōka today, are actually reacting to the rubbish they have seen by many self-proclaimed, self-promoted wannabes, rather than the true Budō practitioners who do so much for the individuals they teach and the community around them. In that, I am in total agreement. But, in the attempt to distance themselves from 'traditional' Martial training, those who concentrate only on the violence aspect, are both irresponsible and just as open to ridicule as those of us who still wear the white pyjamas.

Teach your students to actually fight.

Teach them to work hard to achieve their goals.

Teach them to defend themselves and others, but fight only as a last resort.

Teach them to be better people and help others.

Teach them to work well with and respect others.

Teach them this and whether you wear white pyjamas or a black hoodie….

You are teaching them *Budō*.

Long live Budō

Wabi-sabi

Written by Tony Bailey

Some people see a broken, gnarled, uneven, and aesthetically recalcitrant form, but those same attributes tell a story. They tell the history, trials and suffering endured and more importantly, they tell of a journey of survival through transformation.

As Martial Artists, we are the broken bowl. We harness our skills through years of hard practice, denial, pain, injury, blood, sweat and tears. All the while, whilst our bodies undergo these trials, our mind is sharpened; our emotions are educated and our awareness of our connection to the universe deepens in a truly spiritual way, far older than, and beyond the reach of, Man's invention of dogmatic religion.

We are all on the path of self-discovery. Those who are on the path already, should help others coming up behind them, but, be careful not to rob them of the chance to be transformed by that journey. Pointing out an easier path may not be the kindest thing to do as it may lead to a different destination with far less scope for growth. The way is hard. It is meant to be hard. It is through the hard path that we are transformed. This way is the path we choose, but it is not for everyone. There are always improvements to be made along the way and our efforts often seem short-lived, in a constant state of flux, or forever searching out for that improvement. But be careful. Constantly looking for perfection, you can lose sight of the beauty you've already created.

The Japanese concept of *Wabi-sabi* is based on the understanding;

'Nothing lasts, Nothing is finished, Nothing is perfect.'

Rather than a negative statement, it is a celebration of the perspective which recognises beauty and worth outside of the conventional norm.

Proudly wear your badges of survival in whatever guise they come. Remember the hard work it took to reach every achievement and use that as inspiration to continue during the hard days ahead. Do the best you can for today, as today will never come again. Tomorrow, do the best you can for that day.

Making the most of today, each day, will reveal a different, sobering and valuable perspective of Wabi-sabi:

Everything is perfect, <u>because</u> nothing lasts forever.

Martial equilibrium – Part 1

Tony Bailey

In the Martial Arts world, we see countless references to balance throughout our training life; Yin & Yang, In & Yo, it is the way of the warrior philosopher we are told. It's not unique to any one particular genre as we see it within Japanese, Chinese and even the Indian practices of our distant martial past, but, just how many people, instructors and students alike, understand and practice Martial Equilibrium?

A good martial education could be pictorially represented by that Yin & Yang symbol, which teaches us that a whole is made of 2 halves, a symbiosis of mutual beneficence providing an equal and balanced outcome. It is this balance which mirrors the dualistic nature of even the very universe itself. As Sir Isaac Newton postulated in his 3rd Law of Motion: for every action, there is an equal and opposite, reaction. But, how many of us that study these fighting arts, also study the antithesis that is the spiritual side associated with them? Or even the mental or emotional aspects of training? How many of us take on board and understand these aspects? Putting to good use the discipline, beneficence, mindfulness and harmony intrinsically entwined within many of the stories so often referred to in martial teachings. How many of us try to utilize and incorporate these important principles into our everyday routine both in and outside of the dojo, so as to make a daily advancement in our studies? Are we moving forward each day with our studies, or are we physically, mentally, emotionally and spiritually unbalanced from practicing only a small part of the art we profess to admire and adhere to? Surely, the more we practice and learn about them, these other aspects, the better we are able to understand and correctly apply the physical part of our techniques and more importantly, through a well-balanced outlook, foster a well-balanced *intent* to use them for the right reasons?

During the last 25 years of teaching, I have constantly referred to training within Martial Arts as;

'a spiritual journey of self discovery, through physical means'.

Martial arts, of course, has a necessary physicality to it, but I argue that, if taught and studied in a specific way, the physical is a kind of esoteric teaching which leads the way to an awakening of the student. An epiphany, if you will, as part of the transformation the student undergoes on their journey of self discovery. This, of course is not new news, but the thing I find sad, is that many who study, have no knowledge or interest in these matters. As a consequence, they are only benefitting from a reduced pool of knowledge and experience which could help them to help themselves as well as others.

I am deeply rooted in the Japanese arts, 43 years study to date with Ju Jutsu being my primary interest, but even in my own art, there are vast differences between different schools of thought on this subject. You only have to throw Ju Jutsu into a google search to find several different spellings for a start – Jujutsu, jujitsu, jiu jitsu, even jitz as I believe some in

BJJ are colloquially calling it now, so if we can't even agree on the spelling of our art, how can we have commonality within that which is taught? Well that's kind of the point. There is variance in 'styles' within a common form. Just as within the Chinese arts, different teachers have highlighted specific aspects according to their own preference and different names often signify different styles, albeit related by a common form.

When I speak to students on this topic, I liken Ju Jutsu to Milkshake. Milkshake (Ju Jutsu) is the root and the medium by which different 'flavours' (styles) are delivered or experienced. Let's say you like bananas. Now, banana milkshake from Marks & Spencer, tastes quite different to banana milkshake from McDonalds. It's still banana milkshake even though each brand tastes different, and that's without even getting into the fact that banana is only one of a multitude of different flavours of milkshake available. Milkshake is the form, the flavours are the styles and whilst each style is related to the form and contains most of the same ingredients, each flavour has something of its own which sets it apart from the others, whether it be something added or left out of the original recipe. Once you've found the form and flavour you enjoy, don't forget that even when you've found your favourite flavour, there are several different ways that recipe can be mixed. Each chef or instructor, can use slightly different ingredients, so if you find one which doesn't taste right, don't let it put you off your favourite flavour straight away, search out a different recipe.

To me, the art or form which professes balance within its philosophy, has to have just that. Balance in its teachings, so the form of this type of true training, has to have the ingredients of health, healing, philosophy, morality and ethics as well as the physical fight and exercise training. To this end, I teach aspects of Japanese Reiki to many of my students as one of the ways in which I strive to maintain that balance. In Mizu Ryu Ju Jutsu, after bowing on, all begin their lessons with *Mokuso* (meditation) not just to concentrate on the lesson to be, but to close off and discard what has been, so as to begin training with a clean slate, devoid of the stresses of life outside the dojo and in doing so, attempt to bring a mindful attitude to their training. It's also a mental training for discipline as teaching a 6 year old 'hyperactive' child to sit still for 10 seconds has its own challenges, never mind 10 minutes! But, with the right approach, they not only do it, but enjoy doing it. I find that children especially, take to the healing aspects of reiki without preconception and tend to utilise correct intent. One example I can give is of 2 young girls practicing and one falls a little faster than expected, prompting her to cry from the shock. Obviously checking for injury and finding none, I instruct her partner to sit her down, to sit behind her and to put her own hands gently on top of her head at the crown chakra, to then concentrate on helping her training partner to 'heal' and feel better. After 30 seconds, I observe not only has the crying stopped and the breathing has regulated, but both of them, whilst eyes are shut, are breathing in sync and calm. They are both receiving something from the healing practice. Afterwards I ask the 'practitioner' what she was thinking whilst holding her hands on her partners head and she replies 'I was thinking, be happy, be happy, be happy'.

All Japanese Reiki has a focus on the *Tanden*, the 'centre' where we collect, cultivate and dispense the *Ki* energy. This is by way of meditative breathing exercises and using *intent* to direct it either for ourselves or for the good of other people. *Intent* is the driving force which enables you to do something with this energy. Once we have achieved this centralization within ourselves through this introspective practice, we begin work on integration with others. As, once we are at peace with ourselves, a peaceful integration with others is more achievable. This is just one aspect of creating Martial Equilibrium and its effects reach far further than just within the dojo walls.

We should try to practice this outside of our classes, not just at the dojo, but in everyday life. Mindfulness and meditation are so important and scientifically proven to reduce stress, one of the biggest negative factors in our lives. Be mindful when training – just train, don't think about what you want for dinner afterwards and don't constantly compare yourself to others. Be mindful when walking – just walk and enjoy nature around you, be mindful when washing up….in fact, according to Alan Watts:

'….the art of washing dishes…….. There is only Now. You only have to wash one dish! It's the only dish you ever have to wash! This one!" ...so any task can be training for mindfulness and can be used in a moving meditation.

In 2001, Soen Ozeki the Chief Abbott of the Daitokuji Zen Temple in Kyoto, gave me this teaching which has stuck in my head ever since:

Every day in life is training, training for myself.

Though failure is possible,

Living each moment, equal to everything, ready for anything.

I am alive.

I am this moment.

My future is here and now.

For, if I cannot endure today,

Where and when will I?

We constantly train amid a never-ending search for perfect technique and it is our journey of discovery, trial and error which helps to change and shape us as Martial Artists. The journey changes us. Every day we change in our ability to perform these physical tasks. But, just because we can not always, or never do, perform perfect technique, it doesn't mean that we do not understand it, or recognise it, or should stop trying to achieve it. This helps to foster our *perseverance* in our mental training. Together with the correct *intent,* we can continue to strive for perfection and make a daily advancement in our studies for the benefit of our Martial Arts, ourselves and the people around us. *Perseverance* through *repeated practice* will breed *fluency* and *confidence* in the physical skill, but without the balance of a good *intent*, the technique, good as it may be, is no more than a loaded gun in the hands of a chimpanzee.

'Good technique is useless without the understanding and knowledge of when to and when not to use it.' A subject for further discussion.......

Martial Equilibrium – Part 2

In my previous article, Martial Equilibrium part 1, I was talking about *intent* and I left off with the following statement:

'Good technique is useless without the understanding and knowledge of when to and when not to use it.'

Let's further examine that with some examples. There are many different aspects which can be inferred from this statement, but looking at the 4 main sections of this teaching, it talks of:-

1. Having practiced a technique well enough so you can use it ***fluently*** without stopping,
2. Practicing it within the context of its use under real-time situations so you can get the timing of when and how to use it most effectively, in other words, ***Pressure*** testing.
3. The ***ethical*** aspect of whether it is morally right to use that technique for real, calculating the need to use it against the physical outcome it will have on the person you use it on.
4. Being focussed and situationally aware enough, to handle all the information available to us, and make these difficult ***decisions*** under the pressure of a real threat of violence.

1. Fluency

When we first learn a technique, it takes a certain amount of time to gain fluency within that technique. That time is further augmented by both the inherent difficulty level of the technique as well as the student's ability to understand and replicate what they have been taught. A large part of the responsibility here also lies with the teacher. Just because they are able to perform a technique, it doesn't necessarily follow that they understand how to effectively teach that technique to another person. Understanding how to see from someone else's perspective, or to remember what it felt like for them when they first learned it for themselves, might be something long forgotten. The fluency we seek, is one of the reasons why practical repetition is so important in Martial Arts, as the imperfect maxim 'practice makes perfect' reminds us. In reality, practice doesn't guarantee perfection. Practice improves perception, application and muscle-memory, so the maxim should really be 'practice builds neural pathways', but it doesn't quite have the same ring, does it?

2. Pressure test

Practicing a technique within the context of its use under real-time usage, requires several things: a realistic attack, a realistic environment and a realistic technique. I am very much a traditionalist at heart. I've also spent many years using techniques for real in the real world, and can truthfully say that many of the techniques I've used for real were very traditional. But, there's a great deal of traditional technique that just wouldn't hold up to 21st century scrutiny and usage. There are many different reasons for that. For example, the technique may have been an exercise or teaching aid to understand a principle and never meant for real time usage in the first place. Alternatively, the expected attack and defence known when the technique was first devised, may no longer represent the sum total of knowledge of a 21st century aggressor. This is even more relevant today with the accessibility of UFC and other fight platforms to the masses. These can provide a source of endless study to those who don't train, yet, who can become reasonably proficient with certain techniques against an untrained victim. Either way, with lots of practice building and strengthening neural pathways, you're more inclined to use what you know, so, make sure it's a realistic technique. Fit for purpose. Short and direct. Not extravagant and flamboyant, or your attacker will think he's in bullet time and have loads of opportunities to counter strike.

Make sure when you practice defending a punch to the head, that your partner actually aims for your head, not 6 inches to the side. Lastly, and most importantly, try to recreate the adrenaline filled, mental and emotional minefield of confusion that operating under stress brings us. Those styles that don't do any kind of contact spar training, yet expect to be able to use technique effectively in the real world are, sadly, misguided. The more you practice your techniques under pressure: a non-compliant partner, maybe with distractions, noise, uneven flooring, enclosed spaces, at the point of exhaustion, the more likely you will begin to learn how to make it work, when you need it to.

Any of these aids to training are worth their weight in gold in the preparation for real-time usage. I'm a big proponent of mental preparation. It's hugely important and mustn't be left out, but we're talking about physical skills here, and physical skills need *physical* practice. The best practice at learning to tie your shoelaces, is to practice tying your shoelaces, not to attend seminars on the theory of tying a shoelace whilst never actually touching a shoelace! My friends, you can practice the art of fighting without fighting all you want, but the first time someone smashes you full pelt round the chops, I'm gonna bet, when you get up, you ain't gonna feel like offering them your other cheek! Feeling a physical response, changes your perception of both hazards and risk.

3. Ethics

It's within this last aspect that some will find themselves not paying enough attention during actual conflict and where bravado, negative ego and fear become more visible. Using a technique for real means we have to pay particular attention to the possibilities for either: being able to extend that single technique into a combination if it doesn't have the desired effect, or to stop after using that particular technique if it has achieved the desired effect. Ethics, is concerned with what is morally right and wrong and in our world, it has far reaching legal consequences. As Martial Artists, trained in some of the ancient arts of war, and as compassionate people belonging to the collective of the human race, it is our duty to check this last part thoroughly.

Here is where I depart from many Reality Based Self Defence 'experts' as to me, many I've come into contact with over the years, not all, but many, glorify violence in order to polish their own ego. They do so in order to look good, or to seem tough, but in doing so, they demonstrate unethical behaviour which will be copied by those they teach. When under attack, depending on the severity of that attack, it is as much our duty to protect ourselves, as it is to also protect the aggressor from undue and excessive force due to our own, out of control, negative ego. Now, many would disagree, saying 'well if they attack, they deserve whatever they get!', but that's just playground logic. Whilst little Freddy might very well have pushed John Jr first, would you legitimately stand there and allow John Jr to purposely break Freddy's arm in return? It's overkill, right? No acme of skill, just egotistical, near psychopathic nastiness. It's also not even just a matter of ethics, it's a matter of legality too.

It is our knowledge of technique, the fact that we are trained to do this, which gives us the confidence to act and to be able to choose what to do when under attack. But, it is also our *intent*, compassion and awareness of ethics, which should stop us from going overboard when under attack. Surely all would agree, it must be only the actions of an out of control, selfish, egomaniac who would continue to do more damage than is actually necessary in a situation of self-defence? That is without even looking at the illegality of such an act of overkill, or the fact that self-defence should be about creating an escape from the situation, not standing ground, that's fighting. I'm not talking about turning the other cheek either, we have the absolute right to defend ourselves and even to act first in our own self-defence, we just need to ensure we do enough and not too much. So, in this way, looking after the aggressor is actually looking after ourselves, by not giving in to that 'Red Mist' that would have us go too far and end up being morally and legally worse than the aggressor.

4. Difficult decisions

When that punch is already on its way to your head, there's a lot to think about in a split second isn't there! That's why it is easier to go the peaceful route and try to use other strategies to diffuse or change the situation before it gets to physical confrontation. Situational Awareness plays a huge part here. But obviously, there are times when you don't have a lot of time and you have to act. Believe me, having worked on the door for 3 decades and having some pretty hairy times, I am well accustomed to both worlds. Having experience of people so as to pro-actively pre-empt, rather than re-act to something that has already happened, is something for another time. Just to be clear, I'm not even talking about pre-emptive striking, but pre-emptive strategies, as they can often stop a situation from falling into the realm of physical action.

When it comes to physical action, even though you act in self-defence, you still should be assessing whether what you are about to do is right for the circumstances (*necessary and proportionate*). That's one of the reasons you practice things over and over again. You have to really know a technique inside out, in order to help make the correct decision. Deciding whether to use it or not, in a very short space of time, is not easy. You learn so many techniques that choosing one above others can be difficult, as you can easily second guess yourself. Your training should hopefully lead to the point of *Mu shin* (emptying of the mind). Mushin is not as simple (or as hard) as completely emptying your mind, it's more emptying your mind of distractions. For many, that's both the best and worst part of Ju Jutsu. Learning so many different techniques and practicing so many different ways to use them, then eventually trying to put them all to the back of the mind. The difficulty in achieving that and allowing your sensitivity and experience, governed by your good *intent,* to make the right decision under pressure, cannot be overstated. You don't have time in a real attack, to individually select each technique as if following some predetermined Kata, but you cannot act without considering the ethical and legal consequences of your physical decisions. There's a lot to think about in a short space of time.

But, how do you choose a technique without consciously thinking about it and make sure that it is necessary and proportionate? In reality, there's no shortcut. You need a good teacher, lots of practice, a present mindset and good *intent*.

All this: **fluency**, **pressure testing**, **ethics** and **decision making** in physical technique, all of it makes up just one aspect of Mind, Body and Spirit acting as one, so succinctly immortalised in the words of Spiderman creator, Stan Lee:

'With great power, comes great responsibility'.
(Although I'm pretty sure a dude called Sid said it before him!)

So, back to my original statement:

'Good technique is useless without the understanding and knowledge of when to, and when not to, use it.'

It's now not just a matter of whether I'm good enough to use the technique without making a mistake, or whether I'm quick enough to recognise the opportunity to use it, or whether the technique I choose to do will leave opportunities for a combination, but also, is it morally right to use that technique in the first place? Is it legally right to use it under the circumstances? Is it too much in comparison to the damage or potential damage that could be done to me by the attacker? Should another technique, less physically impacting be substituted or not?

In the UK, the Law *(Section 3, Criminal Law Act 1967)* tells us quite simply that in self-defence, the force we use should be *'reasonable in the circumstances'* and we also find legal descriptions as 'necessary and proportionate'. But what is reasonable? What I think is reasonable and what you think is reasonable might be quite different. As far as the Courts are concerned, the force used for self-defence will be tested under 2 aspects: 1) Whether you did what you truly believed was necessary at the time, based on how you perceived the threat towards you and 2) How what you actually did, would be perceived by others in order to determine the proportionality of that response. A 'Total' defence is reached when the Court agrees with you on both fronts. But it is possible to be right on one and wrong on the other i.e. you might be able to prove you only did what you thought and felt was right at the time, but others might still consider what you did was too much, not proportionate.

Our *intent* helps us to use the technique and make it work, but just as we need physical standards to shape our skill, we also need a moral standard that helps us to choose the right technique in the first place. What are these standards and how do we know them?

We'll look at this in the 3rd part of Martial Equilibrium.

Martial Equilibrium – Part 3

We left part 2 of Martial Equilibrium with a statement – Our intent helps us to use a technique and make it work, but just as we need physical standards to shape our skill, we also need a moral standard that helps us to choose the right technique in the first place. Then the question – What are these standards and how do we know them?

Where do we find the right standards to ensure we are working towards the ideal technique and the ideal version of what a martial artist should be? We have teachers setting examples and organisations setting rules and guidelines, but with so many different teachers and organisations, we don't have complete uniformity of standards there, especially in our world of Martial Arts. We quite naturally take on the ideals of our teachers, but in the greater scheme of things, who's to say those ideals are correct? Everyone will have their own ideals, believing theirs is correct. How many wars, for example, have been started and continued by people who genuinely believed what they were doing was right? Who is to say that my ideals, my standards are correct and better than yours?

The Greek Philosopher, Plato *(428 – 347BCE),* would argue that such ideals or 'blueprints' for standards are held in a kind of cloud bank of knowledge, to which we are all wirelessly connected. The information is already there before we are born as it forms part of a 'mass consciousness' we are all connected to. Plato relates this to what he called the '*Realm of the Forms*'. Although the theory of the Forms was later thrown out by other philosophers, it was again revitalised later. Anyone who's read Tom Campbell's My Big TOE (*Theory Of Everything*), will see its similarities echoed in the Larger Consciousness System that the former NASA Physicist talks about in his theory. For now, we'll use Plato's forms to explain a principle.

Plato asserts that the *physical realm*, our physical world - the matter we experience and interact with each day, is not really the 'real' world, it's a shadow of reality. Instead, ultimate reality exists beyond our physical world in the *spiritual realm* or the *realm of forms*. Here, we find the true reality of perfection outside of the physical realm. It is where the forms for; Roundness, Beauty, Justice, Goodness etc, reside. The physical realm is changing and imperfect, as we know all too well. The spiritual realm, however, exists beyond the physical realm and the incorporeal forms there are perfect, unchanging concepts of truth, which transcend time and space. Our attempts to replicate the best version of something within the physical realm, an *example of form*, doesn't always, or hardly ever, match the actual ideal of that form in its highest and truest manifestation. *(a true martial artist trains in the constant pursuit of perfection, knowing it's unlikely they will ever reach it, yet they still continue to train)*

In a martial sense, our 'form' or standard comes from what our teacher tells us is good, or not, when we are learning and they in turn, received their standard from their teacher, tracing lineage back to the founder or designer of the form in the beginning. We copy the standards of our teachers, hoping they have stayed true to the standards or forms of the founders, but we also learn from physical experimentation and experiential standards which tell us directly and intuitively, when something feels right or wrong. This is described in the *Shu Ha Ri* article (p97) and it is how Martial Arts styles have developed over the centuries. Each successive teacher making their own decision whether to stay true to the form they were taught, or design a new one influenced by their own experiences. That takes time and practice and needs a framework or solid foundation, a form, from which to start. In Ju Jutsu, once we have practiced our skills enough, throwing for example, we begin to develop a certain sensitivity that allows us to make many small changes during the technique. These changes are made according to changes in our opponents' weight, position, resistance etc that our body recognises. As we improve working with our intuition, we account and make adjustments for these changes, without conscious thought. I imagine I'm not alone in the practice of having my own students occasionally train blind fold for that very reason. To take away that sense which we come to rely on so much, so that we may further develop the sensitivity of the other senses. Different types of training exercises can be used to attain the ideal form: some traditional, some modern, but the intended form is the same. There can be many different roads between us and our final destination, each leading to a different journey experience, even if the intended destination is the same. Ultimately, the journey will either get us to the intended destination, or we will end up at a different one, either way, we have been transformed in our pursuit of attaining the ideal standard.

We are fortunate to have good teachers who hand down to us that tried and tested framework from within which we will base our efforts to replicate true form. Like Plato's Realm of Forms, the true framework, the ideal standard handed to us by our teachers, is the form and our physical efforts to replicate it are different *examples* of the form. The *example* of the form isn't the form itself and the form cannot be identified or described purely by looking at one example. (*Much like my analogy of Milkshake and different flavours in part 1 of this article*). The idea of the forms as an abstract truth may still be correct, with an ultimate truth of what martial artist-ness is, residing in the spiritual realm, but our own personal standards, our *example of forms*, tend to be a mixture of;

- practice which we are taught is correct (*fluency*)
- that which we have found by stressful experimentation works (*pressure test*)
- that which we believe intrinsically and morally 'feels' right (*ethics*)
- choosing the right answer, for the right reasons at the right time (*decisions*)

We will never get close to realizing the true form, the ideal technique, if any of these are missing from our studies: Fluency, Pressure test, Ethics and Decisions, just as I covered in Martial Equilibrium part 2. Good teachers are so important in setting out pathways for us to achieve the intended standards. They help us to continue improving both our techniques and ourselves. We constantly train amid this never-ending search for perfect technique and it is this journey of discovery, trial and error which helps to change and shape us as martial artists and as people.

We are transformed by the journey and every day we change in our ability to perform these physical tasks. But just because we cannot always, or never do, perform perfect technique, it doesn't mean that we do not understand it, or recognise it, or should stop trying to achieve it. This helps to foster *perseverance* in our mental training and together with the correct *intent* we can continue to strive for perfection and make a daily advancement in our studies for the benefit of our Martial Arts, ourselves and the people around us.

So, with this in mind, you should accept that it is going to take time to master these skills and enjoy the journey ahead. Continue to train in the techniques that you think you know, as however good we think our technique is, it can ***ALWAYS*** be improved. Don't become impatient in your quest to master techniques as you will focus on negative rather than positive thoughts. The one who says, I learned everything there is to know in 10 years, has not truly learned anything except to polish his own dark sided negative ego. Even when *Carl Jung* (1875 – 1961) said:

"How can I be substantial if I do not cast a shadow? I must have a dark side also If I am to be whole."

He was referring to the fact that we need to acknowledge the dark and use it responsibly, effectively, in a balanced state of equilibrium with the light. If we ignore the dark (*shadow*), Jung says it gets 'blacker and denser' and we become in danger of being overcome by it and projecting it onto others.

'this integration [of the shadow] cannot take place and be put to a useful purpose unless one can admit the tendencies bound up with the shadow and allow them some measure of realization – tempered, of course, with the necessary criticism. This leads to disobedience and self-disgust, but also to self-reliance, without which individuation is unthinkable.'
        - Carl Jung (A Psychological Approach to the Dogma of the Trinity)

As I said in part 1, *Perseverance* through *repeated practice* will breed *fluency* and *confidence* in the physical skill, but without good *intent* and a balanced approach, the technique, good as it may be, is no more than a loaded gun in the hands of a chimpanzee. Remember our common, central theme of equilibrium:

'Good technique is useless without the understanding and knowledge of when to and when not to use it.'

Seek, foster and maintain Martial Equilibrium, endeavouring to make a daily advancement in your martial knowledge.

More Is Not Enough
The Stonemason

There once was a stonemason who was dissatisfied with himself and with his position in life. One day he passed a wealthy merchant's house. Through the open gateway, he saw many fine possessions and important visitors.

'How powerful that merchant must be' thought the stonemason.

He became very envious and wished that he could be like the merchant. To his great surprise, he suddenly became the merchant, enjoying more luxuries and power than he had ever imagined, but soon noticed he was envied and detested by those less wealthy than himself.

A high official passed by, carried in a sedan chair, accompanied by attendants and escorted by soldiers beating gongs. Everyone, no matter how wealthy, had to bow low before the procession.

'How powerful that official is' he thought. 'I wish that I could be a high official'.

Then he became the high official, carried everywhere in his embroidered sedan chair. But he was feared and hated by the people all around.

It was a hot summer day, so the official felt very uncomfortable in the sticky sedan chair. He looked up at the sun. It shone proudly in the sky, unaffected by his presence.

'How powerful the sun is!' he thought. 'I wish that I could be the sun!'.

Then he became the sun, shining fiercely down on everyone. But, scorching the fields, he was cursed by the farmers and laborers.

A huge black cloud moved between him and the earth, so that his light could no longer shine on everything below.

'How powerful that storm cloud is!' he thought. 'I wish that I could be a cloud!'

Then he became the storm cloud. But, as a storm cloud, flooding the fields and villages, he was shouted at by everyone.

Soon he found that he was being pushed away by some great force, and realized that it was the wind.

'How powerful it is!' he thought. 'I wish that I could be the wind!'.

Then he became the wind. Blowing tiles off the roofs of houses, uprooting trees, he was feared and hated by all below him.

But after a while, he ran up against something that would not move, no matter how forcefully he blew against it - a huge, towering rock.

'How powerful that rock is!' he thought. 'I wish that I could be a rock!'

Then he became the rock, more powerful than anything else on earth.

As he stood there, admiring his power and strength, he heard a sound. It was the sound of a hammer pounding a chisel into his hard surface, and felt himself being changed.

'What could be more powerful than I, the rock?' he thought.

He looked down and saw far below him ……………the figure of a stonemason!

My Grandmaster (Soke Dossett) used to say;

'To understand, recognize'. – To understand others, recognize the faults within yourself, then communication between yourself and others becomes more achievable.

I think it can be used with this parable too and in doing so, it mirrors the teaching of the Japanese concept Wabi-sabi:

'Recognize the true beauty of that which is before you, and you will understand how fortunate you are already.'

Ikigai
Tony Bailey

Ikigai is the Japanese concept which means 'a reason for being'. Some equate it to 'the reason you get up out of bed every morning' or more simply, yet profoundly, 'that which makes one's life worthwhile'.

It can take a fair amount of introspective practice to come to realise what your *ikigai* is and in fact it is thought to be such a worthwhile cause to do so, that it is said that discovering your ikigai can bring benefits to all aspects of your life, not just financial but also health and longevity-wise too.

Dan Buettner, reporter for National Geographic, did an extensive study on Okinawa and said that *ikigai* is the reason for longevity in places such as Okinawa and Japan. One of the main reasons for this is the lack, or lessening of, stress, relating to both the workplace and other aspects of daily life. Having studied it, he said people in these areas tended to do work they enjoyed and found purpose within and therefore ended up enjoying it to such a degree that once they got to 'retirement' age, they wouldn't even be thinking about retirement, but would continue to work, doing something they enjoy, for as long as possible.

Ikigai is holding up a mirror to the inner self and then choosing to do something which comes naturally, never forced or coerced, which brings both a feeling of usefulness to the individual and gratitude from those around them. A true sense of living a meaningful life. In a sense then, ikigai is similar in concept to the Indian principle of *Swadharma* – loosely translated as the law of self.

Swadharma is that action which is in accordance with your nature. Something which, because it works to your own skills, talents and nature, enables you to provide a useful service to others through a natural beneficence. Touching, if you will, your true Buddha-nature. Discarding the fear associated with unauthentic thoughts and actions by acting with true compassion from the heart, for the benefit of others. What better way to live life? In true harmony with yourself and others.

The feeling of living out your *ikigai* through your chosen and suited career, not settling for the humdrum day to day existence, finding *Swadharma* and a true harmony to life, has a very real chemical and physiological effect on us, balancing out the secretion of neurotransmitters in the brain such as dopamine and serotonin and contributes to a healthier lifestyle. Studies even show that *ikigai* is associated with longevity among Japanese people.

Like that old maxim says:

'If you can get paid for something you love doing, you'll never work a day in your life.'

A better sense of well-being, benefitting physical, mental, emotional and spiritual health. Isn't that what we profess to work towards attaining through martial practice? So, with Martial Arts training purporting to benefit the individual on physical, mental, emotional and spiritual aspects, surely everyone who studies has worked out what their *ikigai* is? No?

Maybe it's next to meditation in that bin of 'things to do', which we claim to do?
Martial Arts has some of the most diverse, comprehensive and healthy training exercises, but they are not going to help us on any of the 4 aspects of physical, mental, emotional and spiritual if we don't practice what we preach.

In these most trying times, where many have been 'forced' to take time out, to re-evaluate their lives and maybe even to find a new direction in their careers, why not take some time out to meditate and give serious contemplation to identifying your ikigai.

Make your own *ikigai* Venn diagram. Add words or pictures to each area with information from your own pool of skills, talents and passions. Be truthful with yourself. Work towards finding *Swadharma* to benefit yourself and the community within which you live and in doing so, live a healthier, happier and more productive life.
In short, LIVE your life, don't just participate in the game which is merely concerned with existing.

Fill out your Ikigai Venn Diagram

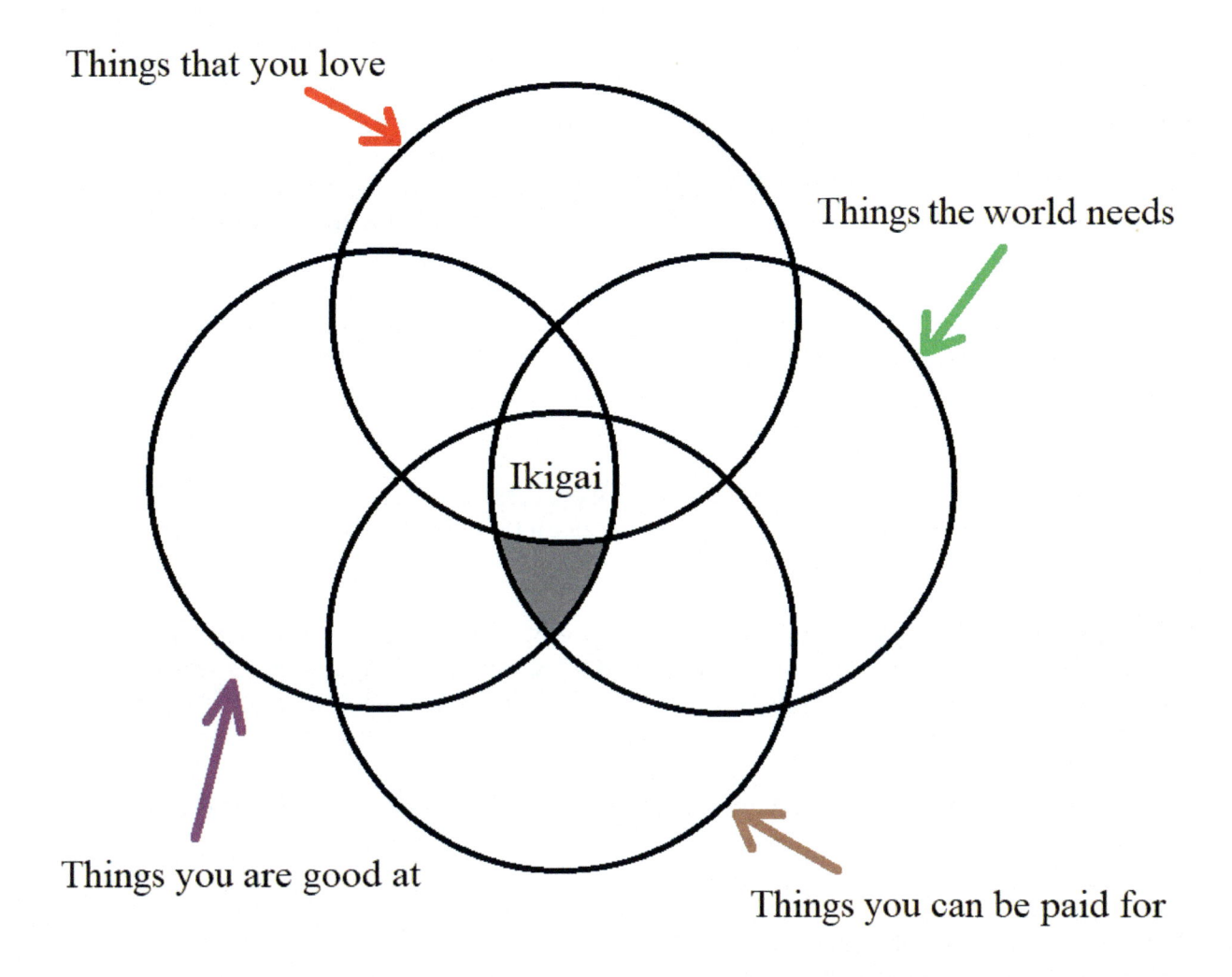

Things that you love

Things the world needs

Ikigai

Things you are good at

Things you can be paid for

On a separate sheet, make a shortlist of answers for each of the 4 headings, then, paying attention to anything which appears in more than one list, put the answers in the corresponding circles.

- **Intersecting Circles**
- Things you are good at + Things you love = Your Passion
- Things you love + Things the world needs = Your Mission
- Things the world needs + Things you can be paid for = Your Vocation
- Things you can be paid for + Things you are good at = Your Profession
- Things which intersect the middle coming from all 4 circles = **Your Ikigai**

This is not professional career advice, but it will help bring several choices, down to just a few, by looking the relationship between your own interests and potential careers.

Mizu Shin

Learn to control your mind.

Your character and temper should develop with training.

Remember the training we put ourselves through, as Martial Artists, is not just physical. We should strive to attain the characteristics of water in our everyday life, as well as in our fighting spirit.

We push our bodies to their physical limits in an effort to attain perfection of technique, but, perfect technique is useless without the wisdom of when to and when not to use it.

There are so many techniques to learn.

If you learn them all and attempt to systematically process each one when under attack, you will fail. You must absorb the techniques and learn to make them part of yourself, put them to the back of your mind and become fluid in your choice of technique.

When sparing or fighting we should have a fluency of movement and thought similar to the motion of water. Giving us the ability to change our technique and thought processes with every change in attack from our opponent and therefore allowing us to make use of each opportunity as it arises.

Only then will you begin to understand the ideal of the Mizu Ryu kanji, which is the symbol of our school.

Mizu is water.
Water is the fundamental essence of life.
Water adapts to its receptacle, as should we to each opponent, and each attack and every problem we encounter in life.

This is the most important teaching of the Mizu Ryu Ju Jutsu school.

Anthony J Bailey, 7th Dan
Founder.

Mizu Ryu Ju Jutsu Emblem

Most organization emblems are simple designs which just create a picture to represent the brand. Ours does that, but there is meaning behind every part of our design which goes deeper into the ethos or philosophy behind our syllabus. A brief explanation for club members follows, but you can glean more information from your own research using this as a foundation.

Mizu Kanji

Directly in the middle, central to our club's existence, the core of the syllabus, is the Japanese Kanji character for *Mizu*, Water. Water here, represents both the fundamental essence of life which nourishes us, as well as the fluidity that we seek both in terms of physical movement and thought response. For more info, read Mizu Shin or the Philosophy of Mizu Ryu Ju Jutsu and its translation, by Master Calligrapher, Eri Takase, Shihan.

Blue triangle

This triangle is the alchemical symbol for water. The Hermetic tradition of alchemy, is most well-known for its scientific pursuit of The Philosopher's Stone. As many teachings are of an allegorical nature, the magnum opus of the hermetic tradition - a transmutation of the prime or base metal through experimentation, into the Philosopher's Stone, can be seen as the personal or spiritual transmutation through hard work, of the raw, untrained beginner into the fully trained and experienced Martial Artist.

2 Pillars

Whilst the base or foundation of the pillars is the same, the tops of the pillars are different. Architecturally, on the left we have the Doric column and Ionic column on the right. Allegorically, they represent 2 different aspects found deep within Martial training – Strength and Wisdom. It is said that the person who brings Strength and Wisdom together, creates beautiful harmony. This is in allusion to the fact that our training must combine not only the physical techniques, but also the knowledge or wisdom of when to and when not to use them.

Yin & Yang

Two diametrically opposed opposites, combining together to make a whole. This signifies the harmony alluded to through the 2 pillars and being in the middle of them, it is the result of that endeavor. It is pictured in the archway, in the middle of the **Key Stone**, cementing its place of pivotal importance as and the piece we seek, which holds it all together.

Taking these elements together, you can see that the emblem speaks of the transformative process that the individual goes through. Through hard work, application, determination, physical, emotional, mental and spiritual work, transforming into someone able to hold all these aspects together, creating harmony both within themselves and for those around them. One of the key principles of Mizu Ryu is found in the words of the founder:

'A person at peace within themselves, can more easily be at peace with everyone else.'

Haiku of Mizu Ryu Ju Jutsu

Fluent as water,
Forceful as the floods of spring.
Flexible response.

This is the haiku of Mizu Ryu Ju Jutsu, as written in 1994.

Haiku, is a type of unrhymed Japanese poem, written in 3 lines with a total of 17 syllables. The first line has 5 syllables, the second line 7 syllables and the third line 5 syllables. It refers to a subject, often of nature, but not always in literal, direct terms.

- **What do you think each line refers to?**
- **How does it equate to the teachings of Mizu Ryu Ju Jutsu?**
- **Why is the principle of this haiku, useful outside of the dojo?**

Mandala

Make copies before you start, in case you want to use the same design in the future

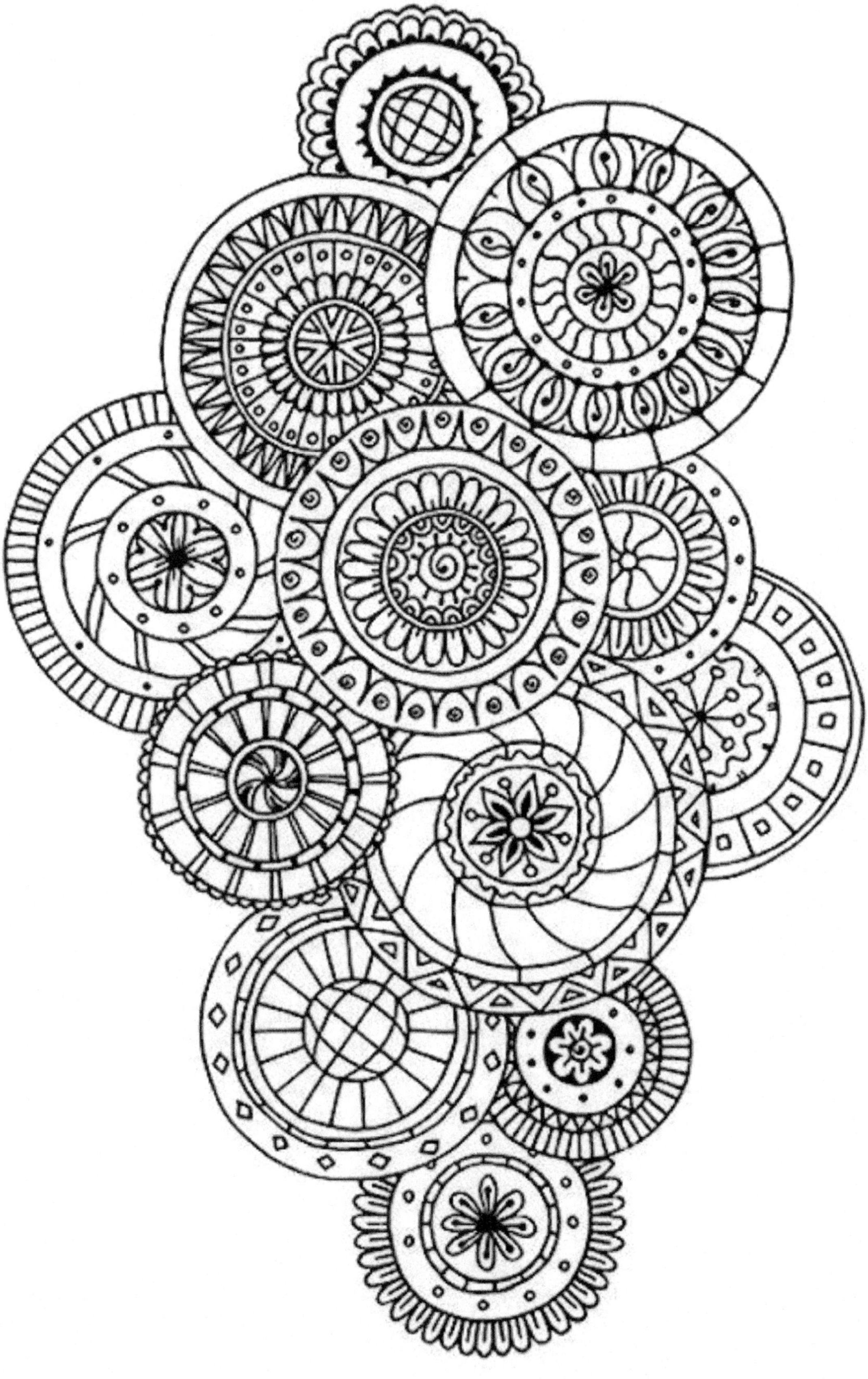

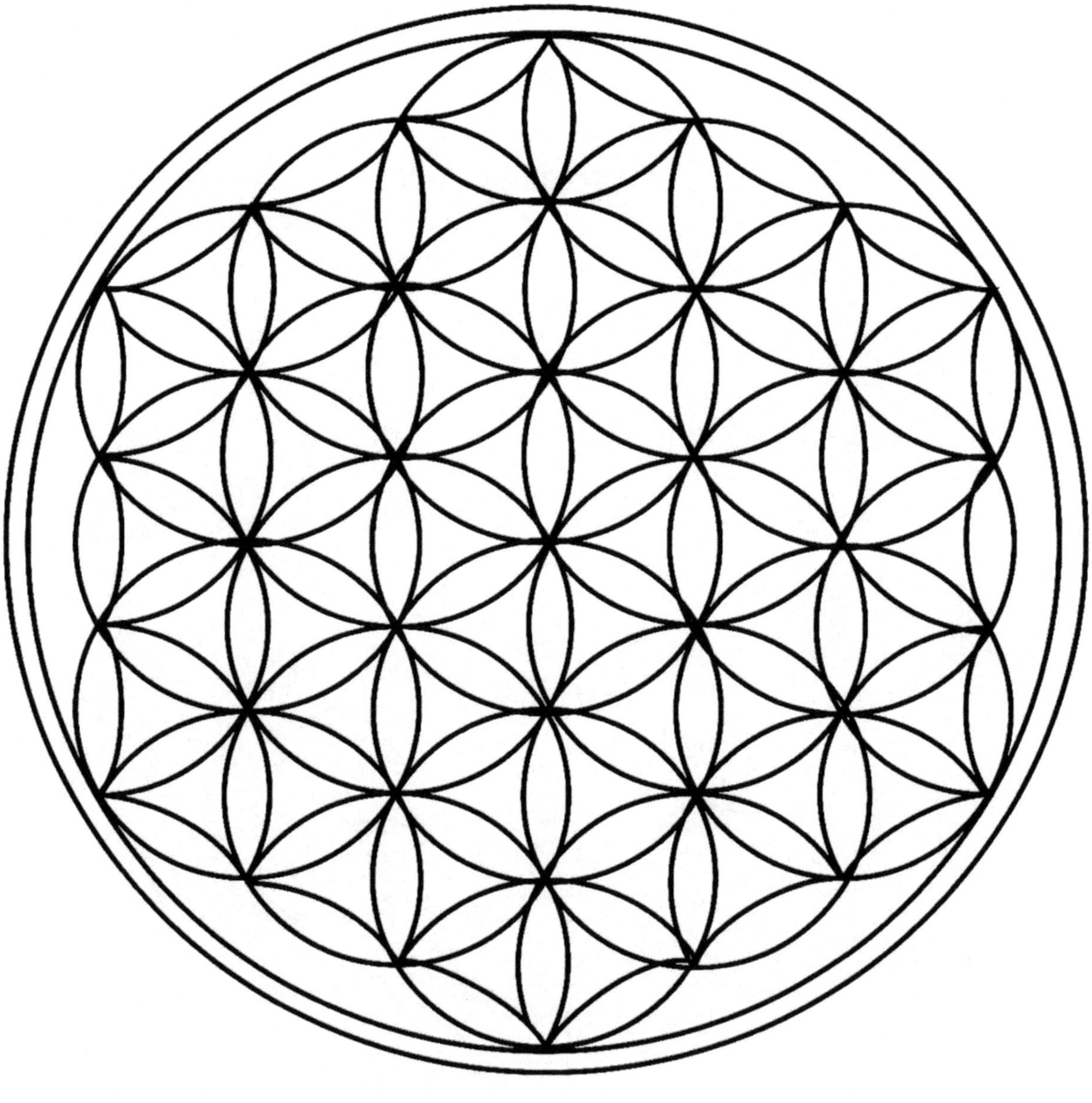

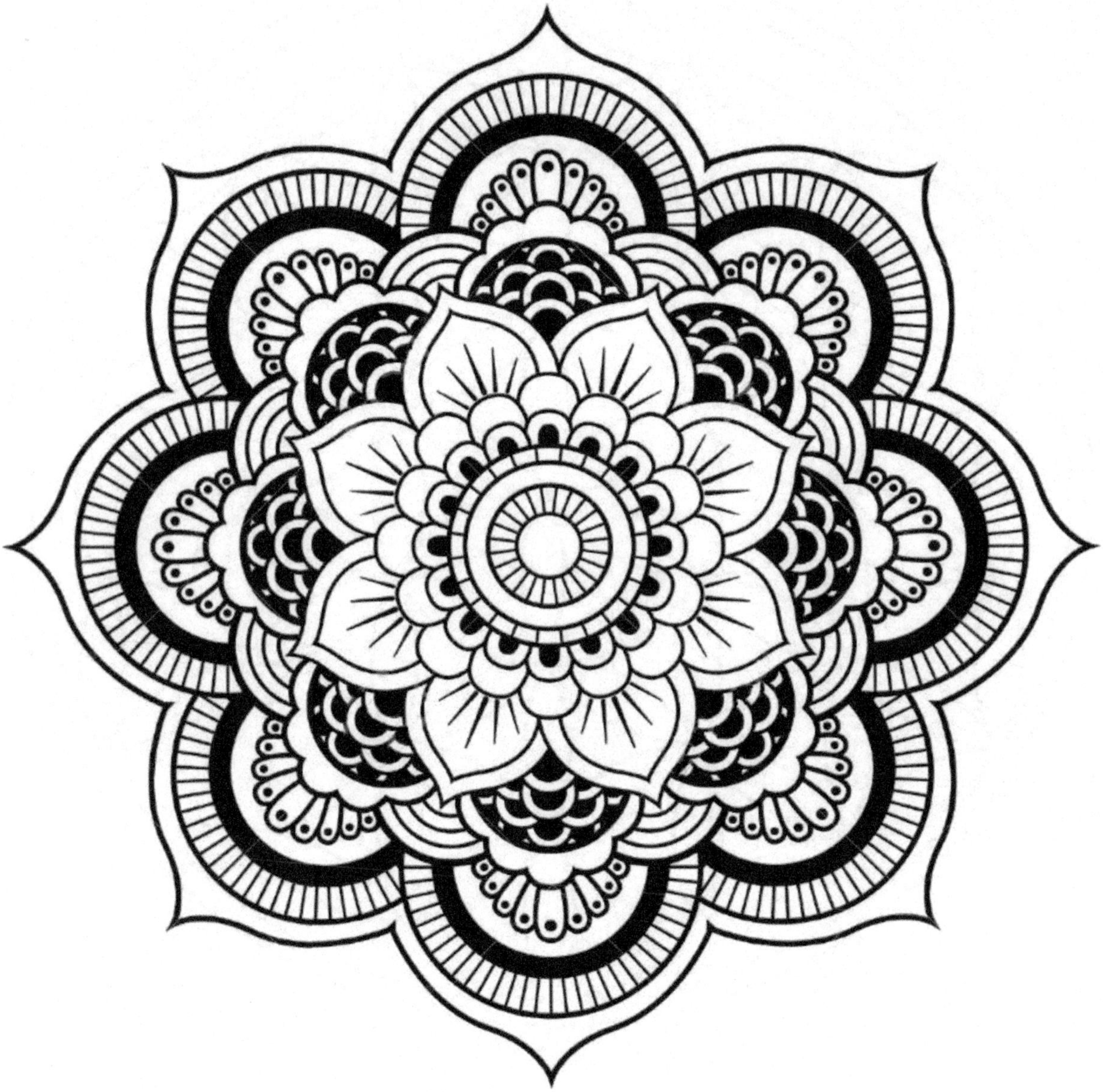

Notes

Mizu Ryu Ju Jutsu

Printed in Great Britain
by Amazon